2009 Poetry Competition
YoungWr...

I have a dream 2009
Words to change the world

Martin Luther King

John Lennon

Poems From Around The UK & Overseas
Edited by Vivien Linton

First published in Great Britain in 2009 by:

Young Writers
Remus House
Coltsfoot Drive
Peterborough
PE2 9JX
Telephone: 01733 890066
Website: www.youngwriters.co.uk

All Rights Reserved
Book Design by Spencer Hart & Tim Christian
© Copyright Contributors 2009
SB ISBN 978-1-84924 408 4

Foreword

'I Have a Dream 2009' is a series of poetry collections written by 11 to 18-year-olds from schools and colleges across the UK and overseas. Pupils were invited to send us their poems using the theme 'I Have a Dream'. Selected entries range from dreams they've experienced to childhood fantasies of stardom and wealth, through inspirational poems of their dreams for a better future and of people who have influenced and inspired their lives.

The series is a snapshot of who and what inspires, influences and enthuses young adults of today. It shows an insight into their hopes, dreams and aspirations of the future and displays how their dreams are an escape from the pressures of today's modern life. Young Writers are proud to present this anthology, which is truly inspired and sure to be an inspiration to all who read it.

Contents

Benjamin Grant 1

Alsager School, Stoke-on-Trent
Alicia Dean (13) 2
Danny Morris (13) 3
Abigail King (13) 4
Becky Preston (13) 5
Katie Sutton (13) 6
Ellie Stevenson (12) 7
Lloyd Downing (12) 8
Charlotte Crook (12) 9
Emma Phillips (12) 10
Sophie Harris (13) 11
Megan Tyler (12) 12
Bethany Anne Edwards (12) 13
Tyrel Stevens (12) 13
Megan McCandless (12) 14
Holly Glenn (12) 14
Joe Webster (13) 15
Bethan Davies (12) 15
Olivia Hollinshead (13) 16

American School of Puebla, Mexico
Adriana Ramirez Mendoza (17) 16
Paulina Chávez Barradas (17) 17
Adam Stansell (16) 18
Miguel Angel Larraza Eden Wynter (17) . 19
Valeria Montserrat Molina Herrerias (16) 20
Angel Francisco Trinidad Rossell (17).... 20
Maria López Villanueva (16) 21
Janina Robles Minutti (17) 22
Felipe Gomez Alvarez (16) 22
Alejandra Ruiz Vega (17) 23
Gerardo De Colombres (17) 23
Jesús Hernández Desiderio (16) 24
Shareni de la Rosa Xochitiotzi (16) 24
Juan Macias Luna (15) 25
Michelle Patricia Loeza Uribe (16) 25

Attleborough High School, Attleborough
Amy Stanton (17) 26
Amy Webb (17) 27
Laurence Grunbaum (17) 28
Frank Garrod (17) 29
Jamie Garwood (17) 29
Rebecca Ashfield (17) 30
Diana Monteiro (13) 30

Bitterne Park Senior School, Southampton
Callula Thornton 31

Cardinal Griffin School, Cannock
Harriet Richards & Megan Shirley (12)... 32
Chelsea Morris (13) 33
Ruth Taylor (11) 34
Grace Bevan (12) 34
Greg Turner (12) 35
Emily Berger (13) 35
Charlotte Hall (12) 36
Lauren Elliott (12) 36
Daniel Hill (11) 37
Eve Gould (12) 37
Steven Ravenscroft (12) 38
Bethany Evans (13) 38
Amy Taylor (12) 39
Jake Jones (12) 39
Imogen Buck (12) 40
Brona Keown (12) 40
Liam Robinson (12) 41
Sebastian Sharratt (13) 41
David O'Rawe (13) 42

Cromer High School, Cromer
Alice Dawson (11) 42
Jordanna Yeo (12) 43
Jack Newton (11) 43
Harry Vanzino (11) 44
Tom Brodie (12) 44

Dorothy Stringer High School, Brighton
Rhoslyn Roebuck Williams (13) 44
Phoebe Dartnell (12) 45
Hannah Clover (12) 46
Miranda Streames (12) 47

Farlingaye High School, Woodbridge
Ellen Lawrence-Clery (11) 48

Grainville School, Jersey
Sophie Fry (13) 49
Ossia O'Donovan (13) 50
Christopher Aubert (13) 51
Sophie Rolland (12) 52
Shannon Hearne (12) 53
Carla De Freitas 54
Katie Fox (13) 55
Curtis Monks (12) 56
Pedro De Abreu (13) 57
Michael Fisher 57
Talluah Brewer 58

Harris Middle School, Lowestoft
Hannah Baldwin (12) 59
Zara Anderson & Shannon Lowe (10) 60
Chanelle Woods (12),
Charlotte Augood & Daisy Gyapong (11) 61
Lola Matthews (12) 62
Shannon Lockwood (12) 63
Lucy Patterson & Rebecca Foster (12) .. 64
Charmaine Allen (11), Neive Banellis
& Sophie Bunn (12) 65
James Hedges (12) 65
Harry Lawrence & Luke Gault (12) 66
Alice Cheverton (12)
& Becky Durrant (11) 67
Ben Cook (11), Darius Mullen
& Joshua Thorpe (12) 68
Nicholas Harrison (11) 68
Lewis Connolly, Elliot Waters
& Paul Tully (12) 69
Michael Mullender (12) & Kim Smith (11) 69
Kelsie Cressy (12) & Lucy Brooks (11) ... 70
Jack Morgan (12) 70

Cameron Moore, Danny Cook
& Liam Bowen (12) 71
Josie McWade & Bethaney Picton (12) .. 71
Sam McMillan (11) 72
Deryn Corbett & Phoebe McCann (12)... 72
Shannon Anderson & Ellie Le Grice (12) 73
Ebony Theaker & Kailey Hugman (12) ... 73

Helenswood Lower School, St Leonards on Sea
Molly Padgham Hugh (13) 74
Shannon Hutchinson (12) 75
Pasha Milburn (13) 76
Isra Husain (13) 77
Jessica Bartlett (13) 78
Laura Kent (11) 78
Samantha Sebbage (14) 79
Bethan Willard (13) 80
Maddie Thomson (13) 81
Jazmin Pook (13) 82
Kathleen Stevenson (14) 83
Georgina Browning (14) 84
Emma Browning (12) 84

Mayfield School, Chorley
Lara Young (11) 85
Ashley Hinds (12) 85
Jessyca Unsworth (12) 85
Natasha Lee (11) 86
Mark Hinds (16) 86
Catherine Reece (12) 86
Kimberley Smith (12) 87
Christopher Macdonald (13) 87

Penryn College, Penryn
Laura Colebrooke (13) 87
Mark Ryan (12) 88
Molly Johnstone-Clark (12) 89
Kai Blackmore (13) 89
Yzobel Wilkinson (13) 90
Michael Snell & Alex Skelton (13) 90
Connor Clements (14) 91
Bethany Wilkinson (12) 92
Kieran Pooley (12) 92
Sam Julian (12) 93

Port Moresby International School, Papua New Guinea
Angela Liu (16) 94
Deborah Nanua (18) 95

Pudsey Grangefield School, Pudsey
Luke Hughes (14) 96
Oliver Bentley (13) 97
Charlotte Thornton (14) 98
Saif Shahidi (14) 99
David Burrell (14) 100
Lauren Berridge (14) 101
Ruth Cass (13) 102
Ben Prest (14) 103
Jessica Sanderson (14) 104
Scott Wilson (14) 105
Lauren Brennan (13) 106
Thomas Johnstone (13) 107
Daniel Sheridan (14) 108
Matthew Christopher (14) 109
Courtney Jade Teale (14) 110
Adam Threapleton (14) 111
Jade Niikole Procter 112

Ratton School, Eastbourne
David Martin (13) 113
Chelsea Willgrass (12) 114
Aidan Pittman (13) 115
Rachel Ledner (13) 116
Polly Davis (13) 117
Jacob Bradbrook (14) 118
Patrick Gates (12) 119
Megan Dennis (12) 120
Lydia Harris (13) 121

Rossall School, Fleetwood
Dominic Baker (14) 121
Aidan Parsons (12) 122
Alex Bettison (12) 123
Ebony Chettoe (12) 124
Sam Lowry (12) 125
Edward So (13) 126
Harry Andrews (12) 127
Jamie Huckerby (12) 127
Dylan Jordan (12) 128

Ella McGuire (12) 128
Lucy Francessca Mary Whalley (12) ... 129
Thomas Gregory (13) 130
Helen Tyler (12) 131
Sera Burney (11) 132
Holly Lawton (12) 133
Harley Taylor (13) 134
Amy Sullivan (12) 135
Lucie Carter (13) 136
Harley Howard (11) 136
Mark Williams (13) 137
Sophie Hockings (13) 137
Bernard Au (12) 138
Joshua Stone (13) 138
Kate Eleanor Chard (11) 139
Ryan Allen (12) 139

Ruamrudee International School, Thailand
Anjida Sripongworakul (16) 140
Madhuri Khanna (17) 141
Penphob Andrea Boonyarungsrit (16) .. 142

Ruzawi School, Zimbabwe
Tom Stubbs (11) 143
Michell Marufu (11) 144
Kimberly Tomlinson (12) 145
Isobelle Pickering (11) 146
Connor Payne (11) 146
Marcus Philp (11) 147
Mathew Ferreira (12) 147
Riaan du Plessis (12) 148

St Peter's High School, Londonderry
Emmett Curran (13) 148
Keaven Brown (12) 149
Caolán Cullen (13) 150

Studley High School, Studley
Rhys Nuttall (12) 150
Amber Yapp (12) 151
Katie Andrews (11) 152
Cara Harrison (15) 153
Alexandra Eaves (14) 154
George Fitzpatrick (11) 155

David Sharples (12) ... 156
Sangamithra Siddhartha (11) ... 157
George Kocon (12) ... 158
Sarah Louise Elmes (11) ... 159
Ben Crossley (13) ... 160
Chloe Greaves (12) ... 161
Tom Daccus (12) ... 161
Beccy Jennings (12) ... 162
Jordon Swingler (12) ... 162
Madeleine Hendy (13) ... 163
Sam Fonyodi (12) ... 163
Connor Brennan (11) ... 164
Joshua Barber (11) ... 164
Elliott Peat (11) ... 165
Georgina Morgan (12) ... 165
Ryan Traves (12) ... 166
Joshua Rogers (12) ... 166
Natasha Carlin (15) ... 167
Joe Moran (11) ... 167
Amy Day (15) ... 168
Callum Grummett (11) ... 168
Amy-Jade Fitter (11) ... 169
Abigail Graham (11) ... 169
Bethany Middleton (11) ... 170
Elliot Evans (15) ... 170
Kyran Flynn (12) ... 171
Caitlin Harvey (11) ... 172
Charlotte Elkins (14) ... 173
Jaspreet Kalsi (11) ... 173
Christopher Sutton-Smith (11) ... 174
Sam Watton (11) ... 174
Vraj Chauhan (11) ... 175
Jake Preece (12) ... 175
Izzy Runacres (12) ... 176
Rebecca Pinfield (12) ... 176
Lauren Shepherd (11) ... 177
Charlotte Roberson (11) ... 177
Oliver Harris (11) ... 178
Heather Paice (13) ... 178
Bradley Maxwell Manchip (13) ... 179
Charlotte Hendy (15) ... 179
David Nuttall (15) ... 180
Olivia Bampfield (12) ... 180
Katie Driscoll (14) ... 181
Benjamin Buffong (14) ... 181

Stacy Archer (11) ... 182
Natasha Vale (12) ... 182
Lauren Rooney (13) ... 183
Rose Morgan (11) ... 183
Gemma Ward (12) ... 184
Bethany Harris (12) ... 184
Max Vanes ... 185
Dan Dowson (12) ... 185
Charley Casey (15) ... 186
Holly Turner (12) ... 186
Ieuan Gibbard (12) ... 187
Daisy Sabin (11) ... 187
Millie Shaw (12) ... 188
Eleanor Oakes (11) ... 188
Lauren Rogers (14) ... 189
Ryan Bourne (12) ... 189
Emily Wood (12) ... 190
Joseph Ashraf-Powell (14) ... 190
Sam Rogers (12) ... 191
Lee Palmer (15) ... 191
Daniel Jackson (11) ... 192
Josh Lawrence (12) ... 192
Charlee Churchill (12) ... 193
Sophia Cleverley (13) ... 193
Hannah Dixon (12) ... 194
Sophia Morgan (15) ... 194
Sam Ali (12) ... 195

The Ladies' College, Guernsey
Emily Green (12) ... 195
Sarah Brereton (12) ... 196
Lauren Nicolle (12) ... 197
Sophie Hunt (11) ... 198
Bethany Schmiedhuber (12) ... 199
Alice Sarre (12) ... 200
Elise Bisson (12) ... 201
Natàlia Tanser (12) ... 202
Lydia Downing (12) ... 203
Anastasia Cross (11) ... 204
Phoebe Morgan (12) ... 205
Fleur Nicolle (12) ... 206
Eleanor Atkinson (12) ... 206
Elise Dorey (11) ... 207
Anna Ogier (12) ... 208
Alice Hudson (12) ... 209

Alisha Crocker (11) 210
Florence Richards (11) 211
Eva James (12) 211

Tomlinscote School & Sixth Form College, Frimley
Bethany Heddle (11) 212
Charlotte Mandell (12) 214
Shira Sokolov (12) 215
Abigail Russell-Samways 216
Brogan McCawley (12) 217
Sasha Mitchell (11) 218
Nicola Evans (12) 219
Emma Walmsley (11) 220
Louise Brisk (12) 221
Hanifah Hashim (11) 222
Ryan Truesdale (11) 223

Uplands Middle School, Sudbury
Yasmine Turner (12) 223

Whitburn CE School, Sunderland
Hannah Woodward (11) 224

Woodbridge School, Woodbridge
Robin Hawes (12) 224
Ella Kiley (11) 225
Saffron Eziashi-Dobie (11) 226
James Davis (12) 227
Adam Lillywhite (11) 228
Louise Fraser (11) 229
Charlie Butt (12) 230
Andrew Norman (12) 231
Elliot Ashurst (12) 232
Olivia Covell (12) 233
Catherine Cooper (12) 234
James Budden (12) 235
Adele Macpherson (12) 235
Molly Fuller (12) 236
Benedict Lelijveld (12) 237

The Poems

Stand Up

The night of eternal darkness will shroud,
The Earth obscured in murky cloud.
Chaos and evil shall surprise,
As darkness falls, a hero must rise!

Fire, water, air and Earth,
All fall at evil's birth.
Chaos and evil shall surprise,
As darkness falls, a hero must rise!

As evil conquers, all will fail,
No such hero shall prevail.
Chaos and evil shall surprise,
As darkness falls, a hero must rise!

At such a heartless sight,
One man will turn and fight.
Chaos and evil shall surprise,
As darkness falls, a hero must rise!

As evil's curse began to spread,
All of humanity turned and fled.
Chaos and evil shall surprise,
As darkness falls, a hero must rise!

The hero travels at a pace,
Blood and sweat pouring down his face.
Chaos and evil shall surprise,
As darkness falls, a hero must rise!

Earth's destruction would come soon,
The final blow, at the full moon.
Chaos and evil shall surprise,
As darkness falls, a hero must rise!

Earth's demise would soon come nigh,
But the fearless hero stood up high.
Chaos and evil shall surprise,
As darkness falls, a hero must rise!

He penetrated evil's heart with a blade,
The great evil had now been slayed,
Chaos and evil shall surprise,
As darkness falls, a hero must rise!

As evil took its last breath,
It turned and fell to its death.
Chaos and evil shall surprise,
As darkness falls, a hero must rise!

How big or scary the evil may be,
You can somehow bring it to its knee,
Chaos and evil had surprised,
As darkness fell, a hero rised!

Benjamin Grant

I Have A Dream

I have a dream,
The world will unite,
Peace will replace war,
Happiness will defeat sadness.

I have a dream,
People will respect one another,
Black or white, man or woman,
Life will be blissful and carefree.

I have a dream,
People will no longer fight,
They will no longer cry,
Unless they're tears of joy.

I have a dream,
There is no jealously,
Or hatred,
People walk hand in hand,
I have a dream!

Alicia Dean (13)
Alsager School, Stoke-on-Trent

I Have A Dream

I have a dream, just maybe if?
This cruel world would alter or shift.

Every time I look, every time I turn, things aren't right,
These people must learn,
These humans don't give me anything good, just concern.

And when I look up into the star fields of the midnight sky,
I can see the beauty, but down here I don't, I just sigh,
Because all I can see is humans kill, torture and lie.

I have a dream, just maybe if?
This cruel world would alter or shift.

Within this darkness I am trapped, surrounded by evil and scandal,
Maybe this world's too much to handle,
I look to my faith, I ask, where's my lighting candle?

There's no escape from this abyss,
My dignity and happiness and sanity I miss,
Oh what I would do for that pure angel's kiss,
There's no escape from this abyss.

I have a dream, just maybe if?
This cruel world would alter or shift.

All I want is a tranquil planet,
But I am driven crazy, I scream, I damn it,
But still I'm stuck, my voice is unheard,
I'm confused, this world's absurd.

Is it too much to ask? Just one minute of silence,
Just stop the shouting, just quit the violence,
I will keep trying, I still have hope,
Yet I know in myself I am lying.

I call forth once more, on my belief I'm relying,
Because it's either this, or joining in or just dying.

I don't know what else to say, the darkness is coming,
I command it to go away,
Now you will listen to me.

I have a dream, just maybe if?
This cruel world would alter or shift.

Danny Morris (13)
Alsager School, Stoke-on-Trent

I Have A Dream

I have a dream,
A place for me,
That no one else will see,
A special wish,
A fantasy,
Where what I want will be.

I have a dream,
Where pigs will fly,
And donkeys can say, 'Hi!'
There are miracles,
A purple sky,
And no one wonders why.

I have a dream,
I'll oversee,
A world of joy and glee,
It's where there is,
No poverty,
So no one's unhappy.

I have a dream,
A magic door,
Through which there is no war,
A place of peace,
In which I saw,
That worries were no more.

I have a dream,
Will you help me,
Make this reality?
Then people will
Wake up and see,
What our Earth could be.

I have a dream.

Abigail King (13)
Alsager School, Stoke-on-Trent

I Have A Dream

I have a dream,
That every day children across the world will wake up,
Pull back their clean bed linen
And breathe in the fresh air surrounding them.

I have a dream,
That Third World countries don't exist,
And water gushes from taps and wells,
No matter what country you are in.

I have a dream,
That no one is scared to go out after dark,
And that knife crime is a long ago ritual.

I have a dream,
That the skies will be sparkling crystal clear,
And global warming is an old wives' tale.

I have a dream,
That black and white people will work together,
And that racism never happened.

I have a dream,
That no matter how old you are,
You are not scared to go to school or work,
And bullies are just mythical creatures.

And finally,
I have a dream,
That the world will see things,
In the same light,
From the same angle,
In the same way.

And war is just a legend,
A dusty, ancient myth,
Just a story in a book.

Becky Preston (13)
Alsager School, Stoke-on-Trent

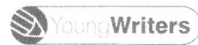

I Have A Dream

Poverty, bullying, sexism,
Death, illnesses, racism.

This world is far from perfect,
That fact, I know, is true,
But now I have a new dream,
A dream involving you.

My dream is not that simple,
But astonishingly clear,
I want a world of peace and love,
Not cruelty and fear.

Abuse is all around us,
A fact we can't deny,
But we can help to stop it,
And tell racism, 'Goodbye!'

Imagine getting out of bed,
To a world that's pure,
Wouldn't it be wonderful?
Yes, it would, I'm sure.

But what can we do?
What can we do?
Just be a good person,
You know it's true.

Poverty, bullying, sexism,
Death, illnesses, racism.

This world is far from perfect,
That fact, I know, is true,
But now I have a new dream,
A dream involving you.

Katie Sutton (13)
Alsager School, Stoke-on-Trent

I Have A Dream

I have a dream,
That one day this war will conclude,
I will at last rest in peace,
Leave the battlefield in utter harmony,
My time having come.

I have a dream,
Soon I will be released,
A free spirit roaming the skies,
Everlasting, inevitable happiness,
No qualms, hopes or fears,
No pain.

I have a dream,
One day, reunited with my kin,
Witness the joy and tranquillity on their faces,
See the pleasure in their eyes,
Watch the worry fade away.

I have a dream,
But alas, it may never come to pass,
Many obstacles guard it, protect it,
Forbidding me to touch it, smell it, marvel its beauty,
I must pass a test,
Win their approval,
To access my only dream.

It may never come,
I might never succeed,
Spending eternity knocking on those wrought gates,
Begging; begging for one thing,
To have my dream.

Ellie Stevenson (12)
Alsager School, Stoke-on-Trent

I Have A Dream

Dreams, they are such magical things,
We have them at any time of day or night,
They give us mysteries,
They give feelings,
We wonder about them,
Was it real?
Was it the future?
Or, was it the past?
We forget about them,
Something reminds us about it,
We share it with others,
Others share it with us,
Some make us happy,
Some make us scared,
Some make us sad,
Others remind us of things from the past,
People love them,
Others hate them,
People ask about them,
You ask others about theirs,
We hate it when one ends,
We love it when one ends,
'Why did it happen?' you ask yourself,
We don't know why we have them,
It's just a matter of time until we find out.

Lloyd Downing (12)
Alsager School, Stoke-on-Trent

I Have A Dream

I have a dream,
That one day the yellow beach ball which hangs in the sky,
Goes black.

I have a dream,
That we will wake up in another world,
A world where things have gone wrong.

I have a dream,
That there will be a day,
A day when we live underwater.

I have a dream,
That all children will be crying,
Crying because they have lost their furry friends.

I have a dream,
A dream where people are killed,
But they have done that themselves.

I have a dream,
When one day you turn on the light,
Only to find it doesn't work.

I have a dream,
People have remembered what happened,
They remembered but there is nothing that they can do.

Charlotte Crook (12)
Alsager School, Stoke-on-Trent

I Have A Dream

I have a dream that one day . . .

Nobody will be judged,
By the way that they look,
Everybody will be judged,
By what they are inside.

For it is the inside that counts.

I have a dream that one day . . .

Nobody will want to fight,
Others that have done no wrong,
Everybody will be peaceful,
And calm and settled down.

For fighting does not solve anything.

I have a dream that one day . . .

Nobody will have to experience,
Hatefulness, jealousy or pain,
Everybody will only experience,
Love, friendship and kindness.

For everyone should be friends.

I have a dream.

Emma Phillips (12)
Alsager School, Stoke-on-Trent

I Have A Dream

I have a dream,
That is special to me,
It cannot be worn,
Can't be bought with a fee,
It stays strong in memory.

I have a dream,
That is special to me,
It springs with life,
Wide and free,
Always in my memory.

I have a dream,
That is special to me,
No more pain,
Nothing bad to see,
Fixed into my memory.

I have a dream,
That is special to me,
A better world,
For people to be,
Can't be moved from memory.

Yes I have a dream.

Sophie Harris (13)
Alsager School, Stoke-on-Trent

I Have A Dream

Some may call me a dreamer,
And I guess I'd have to agree,
But I'd rather dream my life away,
Than live in reality.

In my dreams I can fly away,
And forget this troubling life,
I soar away completely free,
Of all this anger and strife.

In my dreams I'm Superwoman,
Defeating all the bullies,
But I know when I wake up,
I'll still have all these worries.

In my dreams I'm happy,
Happy and carefree,
But in my heart of hearts,
I know it's different in reality.

Some may call me a dreamer,
And I guess I'd have to agree,
But I won't give up trying,
To make my dreams a reality.

Megan Tyler (12)
Alsager School, Stoke-on-Trent

I Have A Dream

One life,
One chance,
One hope,
One dream,
So accept this,
My dream.

To fly high,
Up in the clouds,
Or floating around in outer space,
What a wonderful world,
Such a wonderful place.

Yes, I've been told I'm a dreamer,
And I totally agree,
This world must be a lot better,
Than plain old reality.

My dream may seem whacky,
And I definitely agree,
But my dream is just all about *me!*

Bethany Anne Edwards (12)
Alsager School, Stoke-on-Trent

I Have A Dream

I have a dream that the world will be at peace,
I have a dream that the hunger shall end,
I have a dream that flowers shall wave and bend,
I have a dream that poverty shall cease,
I have a dream that the world shall come to order,
I have a dream that countries shall have no border,
I have a dream that people shall be accepted,
I have a dream that the world will be together,
I have a dream that none will even harm a feather,
I have a dream that the world shall be perfect.

Tyrel Stevens (12)
Alsager School, Stoke-on-Trent

I Have A Dream

I have a dream to end all suffering in the world . . .

Earthquakes cause havoc, mayhem and pain,
Fighting against nature is a losing game.

Floods cause worry, tension and stress,
Leaving homes in a terrible mess.

Disease is common, far and wide,
Help or be selfish, it's for you to decide.

Murder and knife crime can always be stopped,
That bubble of suffering is soon to be popped.

These things need stopping; we should stand our ground,
Stand up, be strong and gather around.

So suffering is harmful, pointless and off beam,
We should respect each other and let that be seen.

So I have a dream, that suffering will cease,
So we can then live in harmony, love and peace.

Megan McCandless (12)
Alsager School, Stoke-on-Trent

I Have A Dream

I have a dream,
I hope for it, I long for it,
I desire it, I crave it,
I query if it could be reality,
It's eternally on my mind,
My Pluto in the planets,
My castle in Spain,
My castle in the air,
My dream.

Holly Glenn (12)
Alsager School, Stoke-on-Trent

I Have A Dream

I have a dream
I will play for Stoke City one day
And all my friends will watch me play
I will be the best defensive player
And as popular as our town mayor
We will play in red and white
And the strip will shine like a knight
I will play until the end
Being a great legend
My debut will be against Man City
But we will win as they're such a pity
I will play until I'm old
When the pitch will grow some mould
I hope you will have a dream
And play for your best team.

Joe Webster (13)
Alsager School, Stoke-on-Trent

I Have A Dream . . .

I have a dream,
A dream that wrong is right,
A dream the world wasn't so tight,
A dream that they would not kill,
A dream nobody would be ill,
A dream nobody should fight,
A dream that life would be light,
A dream that people would not be snatched away,
A dream that I do not want to go away,
But now I wake and go back,
To the life I just want to give up,
If only my dreams were reality,
I would be very, very happy.

Bethan Davies (12)
Alsager School, Stoke-on-Trent

I Have A Dream!

I have a dream for equality,
For you, for her, for him and me,
I want equal rights in every way,
I believe it's called 'Democracy'.

Age, colour, race or creed,
Equality is what we need,
My dream is one I can share with all,
So we can all be proud, and walk tall.

My dream is full of hope and thought,
It comes from within, it cannot be bought,
I hope I live to see my dream come true,
For her, for him, for me and you.

Olivia Hollinshead (13)
Alsager School, Stoke-on-Trent

Just Waiting . . .

Some people wait a lifetime . . .
For a moment of hope,
Others look forever,
To find peace in their souls,
Some people just want
To harm others,
The suffering of others,
This feeling
Moves everything,
Just waiting for a change . . .
A glow of light . . .
Change the world with hope,
Just hope . . .
Some people wait a lifetime,
For a moment of peace.

Adriana Ramirez Mendoza (17)
American School of Puebla, Mexico

Correspondence

Dear World,

Do you ever cry?
Every morning that I wake up, I look into your eyes,
Confused,
I don't know what path I should take,
My wrong steps became sunshine;
Rainbow colours make me one,
Numbers become people,
I lose myself in this hole,
There is darkness on my soul.

Dear Boy,
One day you will find your way,
To imagine
The impossible
Move on
No matter what happens,
Never look back,
All the chaos stays behind,
The good is in your heart,
Don't give up,
Fight for what you want,
Don't let ignorance stop you
And don't be afraid,
Watch the sunshine,
Smile to life,
Be thankful for what you have,
Learn about your mistakes,
People are afraid to speak out loud,
To express what they feel,
Don't let it happen,
You can change me.

Paulina Chávez Barradas (17)
American School of Puebla, Mexico

I Have A Nightmare

I have a nightmare.
The worst part about it
Is that when I wake up nothing's changed.
But in my nightmare
The world is controlled by greed.
Humans have forgotten how to feel,
And have learnt how to run from their emotions.
This world is a cold, pitiless shell.

Then the dream changes,
And now the cold clench of fear slowly releases its grip
Because humans remember how to feel.
They have been inspired,
Awakened.
They have united.
A leader has emerged
Who inspires people to feel again
Feel pride in their country.
He has united the country,
And realigned the country,
The nightmare is over.

But then it returns.
This same leader has fallen short.
He had become the manifestation of human hope,
And disappointed those he had inspired,
And so the negative feelings continue.

Every night
The dream and the nightmare share my subconscious mind
As they share a potential future.
And it's anybody's guess
Which one I'll see when I wake up.

Adam Stansell (16)
American School of Puebla, Mexico

Giggle Discrimination

Here it goes again . . .
Madness flows through my veins,
Desperate sensations dancing through my body . . .
Laughing at me,
Making me want to explode,
But can't do it,
Can't understand their purpose . . .
Their jokes,
Their stereotypes,
Through my anger, a grin appears on my face,
Now I think about it, it looks funny,
Think I even could laugh louder than them,
My purpose is clearer,
I can't understand their purpose . . .
But maybe I shouldn't,
Really shouldn't care,
They'll receive their own punishment,
Blind themselves,
So keep on doing it and tell me what you want,
Laugh at me,
Point the finger,
Intimidate me,
Make a show out of me,
But look at you first,
You will see a bigger show,
'Cause I'm enjoying it now,
Come on, make me laugh . . .

Miguel Angel Larraza Eden Wynter (17)
American School of Puebla, Mexico

Completely

The grass is green - pure green,
People are living with each other,
Sharing, interacting in peace,
Enjoying unity,
Feeling freedom,
Feeling themselves.

It is a shame,
So lame,
A new era,
Supposedly a new world,
And we still suffer,
We can't agree to have differences,
Can't stay forever in the same room.

King gave his life for change,
Yet we are full circle,
Gandhi, Martin Luther King, Simon Bolivar, Che Guevara,
Tried to make their changes,
And they achieved it,
But not completely.

Valeria Montserrat Molina Herrerias (16)
American School of Puebla, Mexico

Match Point

Search for the light, glory ever mine,
Stepping down, but reaching the sky,
I release a power reflected by the other side,
Only one more, shake and go.

Angel Francisco Trinidad Rossell (17)
American School of Puebla, Mexico

Blind Guy

I want to open my eyes,
I haven't seen colours yet,
I dream of a world,
Where people hold hands to cross the street,
My skin is black but I haven't seen it yet,
We're not different,
I'm blind but I might
See clearly soon, if the clouds move away from the sun,
I'm afraid I won't ever see the sun,
Ignorance is thick and will not move easily,
Black labels, define me,
I sense an arrogant world,
People walking through,
No feelings, no joy,
Emptiness defines them,
Colours? What are they? Black? Pink? Purple?
I don't see them,
What colour are you?
I'm black, the colour of shame, or the colour of a pure soul?

Maria López Villanueva (16)
American School of Puebla, Mexico

I Have A Dream

I have a dream,
A world with mercy,
I have a dream,
A sign of destiny,
I have a dream,
Nothing but have him back,
Is the only thing I ask,
From life to pay me back.

This is me,
This is who I am,
He's the one I love,
I'm the one he loves,
I know he'll be back in no time,
Five years seems so far,
But I'll wait in silence,
Knowing my heart,
Will always be true.

Janina Robles Minutti (17)
American School of Puebla, Mexico

Looking For Someone

I stopped breathing, when they were trying to silence me,
Couldn't see what was happening,
I needed a hero,
We all need heroes,
Don't close your eyes or shut your mouths,
Speak up, tell the truth,
Don't close your mind, open your heart,
Follow your words to the lead of achievement,
Follow your heart to the lead of happiness,
Never stop walking, keep on going,
Stop the killing, help a brother,
Make love not war.

Felipe Gomez Alvarez (16)
American School of Puebla, Mexico

River Of Dreams

I want a new hope,
Something to start again,
I would give my life,
My soul,
For a new dream,
Because life isn't enough,
If I could, I would give,
All the money in the world,
Just for a day . . .
Just for one dream,
I see my life slip from the edge,
I see my dreams flow away,
Like a river,
I can't turn back,
I won't stand it.

Alejandra Ruiz Vega (17)
American School of Puebla, Mexico

Why Can't We?

Why can't we
Live like brothers,
No gunshots,
Helping others blindly?

Imagine,
Watching good news,
Where wars, casualties and crimes don't exist.

Why can't we,
Wake up every day, not worrying about thieves?

Respect, tolerance, love,
These are the words the world should be practising,
Every day I ask myself,
Why can't we?

Gerardo De Colombres (17)
American School of Puebla, Mexico

Sleep, Awake, Sleep Again

Tonight I will sleep,
Dream of a world,
Without war, in harmony, peace and love,
But then I will awaken to reality,
Outside soldiers are killing innocent people,
Tanks on the streets, and
The sound of the guns being fired,
I try to get back to that
Wonderful dream,
Instead I hear a jet,
The sound of bombs,
Then I awaken and I am in my
Wonderful world.

Jesús Hernández Desiderio (16)
American School of Puebla, Mexico

What A Wonderful Place . . . In My Dreams

Want to know where I live?
I live in a place where peace rules,
Where wars are over and done,
Weapons are forgotten,
Equality is number one,
Racism is past,
There's no more hunger,
No more conflicts,
Problems are resolved by talking,
And everyone is one big, happy family,
Where respect, honesty and tolerance are main priorities,
Obviously I live in my dreams,
Yet unreachable so it seems.

Shareni de la Rosa Xochitiotzi (16)
American School of Puebla, Mexico

Pure Bred Motorcycle

Going so fast, you feel you're flying,
A nice 1200 cubic centimetre engine,
Enough power to reach 260km/h,
Feeling as if you are in a race between leopards,
Looking at the highway, getting smaller,
Dreaming of paradise,
A dream achieved without killing,
Without extinction,
Chemicals,
Without making life shorter,
Clouding other's lives,
Without losing our human nature.

Juan Macias Luna (15)
American School of Puebla, Mexico

Hope Is The Right Path

When life seems hard and there's no way out,
Hope is the right path,
I dream of conquering hunger and injustice,
Of a world where peace can be seen,
Where men act human,
No suffering, no crisis,
No wars fought,
I have a strength inside that will not run and hide,
A shining star,
That keeps faith alive,
Everything is possible,
If you believe.

Michelle Patricia Loeza Uribe (16)
American School of Puebla, Mexico

My Mummy

Although I may be only four,
When I grow up, I know exactly who I want to be,
Not a nurse, not a teacher, not a vet, not a dancer,
I want to be just like my mummy.

You may wonder how I already know,
But with a mummy like me, I have no doubt,
When she's the queen of my heart.

Her beautiful face brings comfort to me,
In both times when I'm down and when in glee,
Big blue eyes like the ocean sparkling in the summer sun,
Glittering and full of life,
Plump, pink lips that sing me sweet lullabies when I sleep,
And put a smile back on my face when I begin to weep.

Being in my mummy's arms is the very best place to be,
It's warm, cosy and the safest place to me,
When she wraps me in her arms, I know I'll come to no harm,
The reason being my mummy's my very lucky charm.

She has a voice as sweet as honey, as soft as silk,
As soothing an my old 'blankey',
Providing me warmth and comfort and fun,
That's the reason why I know my mummy is the one.

My mummy makes me so proud,
She stands right out from the crowd,
Just like the brightest star in the midnight sky,
Like the first bloom in the spring.

So that is why I know exactly who I want to be,
I want to be just like my mummy,
The perfect angel that she is to me,
I really am the cat who got the cream,
And that is why *I have a dream!*

Amy Stanton (17)
Attleborough High School, Attleborough

I Have A Dream

To those people,
Who survived the dreaded camps
And managed to light candles to remember,
Those who perished alongside them,
Their dreams of freedom were ignited into life.

To those people,
Who fought for their equal rights,
As generations before them had attempted
And as Obama was elected president,
History admired thousands of people's dreams.

To those people,
Who battled pain for victory,
Breaking through barriers as friends and family watched,
And greeted their Olympic gold,
As people gazed on to see their dreams laid bare.

To those people,
Who have been met by terror,
As they reach the handle they are sparked with fear,
But have come out the other side,
And been met with their dreams of breaking through Hell.

Now to myself,
My dream is much more simple,
I just wish for a constant supply of hope,
As it is hope that pulls you through,
And will allow everyone to live their dreams.

Amy Webb (17)
Attleborough High School, Attleborough

Realistic

In my dreams, I see a boy who
Is scared about his differences, a boy
Who fancies other boys, he will be hurt,
Realistic?
A world where I am not ignored,
I am accepted, not tolerated,
Supported, not let down, but respected,
Realistic?
A dream without any whispers,
About queer or faggot or poof,
But still ignored, let down, the token gay,
Realistic?
And teachers don't help; they just make it worse,
'Knowing' what it's like, to be bullied,
Because of nature, my sexuality,
Realistic?
Ninety-four per cent will read this,
But the other six will understand it,
Straight - don't even try to understand it,
Realistic?
In my dreams, I saw a boy who
Was scared about his difference, a boy
Who fancied other boys, he has been hurt!

Laurence Grunbaum (17)
Attleborough High School, Attleborough

I Have A Dream . . .

Maybe one day I won't hide,
Like the sun behind the grey clouds,
Maybe one day it will go away,
Like the birds in the sky just fly,
Maybe . . .

Maybe one day I won't run,
Like an animal in the wild,
Maybe one day I will be free,
Like the slaves when they were released,
Maybe . . .

Now today I don't have to hide,
The sun appears from the grey clouds,
Now today I am free from all cares,
Like an addict hooked on his craze,
I have a dream.

Frank Garrod (17)
Attleborough High School, Attleborough

I Have A Dream

The world is turned upside down,
Racism the main talking point,
Blacks, whites, ethnic minorities,
People running, screaming, shouting,
Different religions, different views,
Suicide bombers everywhere,
People scared, frightened, petrified,
Anxiety, aggression, antagonism,
The world is turned upside down.

I had a dream!

Jamie Garwood (17)
Attleborough High School, Attleborough

I Have A Dream

Daydreaming about the years to come,
My thoughts drift to what will be done,
Our dreams could change,
Like the leaves on trees.

Possibilities and prospects,
Cross our minds,
How things tend to turn in periods of time.

Where would a person be without dreams or desire?
They are what sets us alight as people,
To drive us like a raging fire.

Wondering what the future holds,
Is all of this just a fantasy?
Or will one day,
My dreams become reality?

Rebecca Ashfield (17)
Attleborough High School, Attleborough

I Have A Dream!

I have a dream to be with you,
I hope you are with me every minute,
Do you feel the same for me too?
Love is not far away but you are,
It doesn't matter you are in my heart,
Always and always you are inside me,
Your love I will have every single minute,
No one is more important than you,
You are my heart and soul and my life,
The best dream that becomes reality,
My love for you is stronger than anything,
This is the dream I have and the one I will
Never forget for the rest of my life,
This dream is for eternity!

Diana Monteiro (13)
Attleborough High School, Attleborough

Untitled

I want the dream,
The crouching tiger never jumps,
The leaping deer never lands,
Violence killed them,
Will violence ever end?
Violence ends, joy begins.

I want the dream,
The choking child never stops,
The bleeding victim never stands,
Violence killed them,
Will violence ever end?
Violence ends, grief begins.

I want the dream,
The sleeping kitten never wakes,
The burning tree never revives,
Violence killed them,
Will violence ever end?
Violence ends, recovery begins.

I want the dream,
Filthy air clears,
Needless killings stopped,
Hope freed them,
Will violence ever end?
Violence ends, joy begins.

Callula Thornton
Bitterne Park Senior School, Southampton

I Had A Dream (Can You Paint The Picture?)

Imagine
A place where world hunger came to an end
Imagine
All your troubles going round the bend.

Can you paint the picture?

Imagine,
The call of death never coming,
Imagine,
All children laughing and humming.

Can you paint the picture?

Imagine,
Poverty disappearing in the air,
Imagine,
The unfortunates never getting the stare.

Can you paint the picture?

Imagine,
If colour didn't matter,
Imagine,
If starving kids get fatter.

Can you paint the picture?

I had a dream the world was perfect all through,
But unfortunately some dreams never come true.

Harriet Richards & Megan Shirley (12)
Cardinal Griffin School, Cannock

I Have A Dream

I have a dream,
Love and peace in the world,
Parents have a boy or girl,
Everyone has a lover,
Caring for each other,
Money growing on trees,
With pretty bumbling bees.

I have a dream,
Massive candy stores,
With chocolate tasting doors,
Tall, scary rides,
Scared out of your lives,
No homework at all,
Big shopping malls.

I have a dream,
Me to be a great dancer,
Me becoming a brainiac master,
Me succeeding all my dreams,
Hope that I never become mean.

But my biggest dream of all,
Is for this world, to bring happiness,
To big and small.

Chelsea Morris (13)
Cardinal Griffin School, Cannock

I Have A Dream!

My dream is this . . .

The blind will see,
The deaf will hear,
The dumb will speak,
The lame will dance.

I have a dream,
That children will play, and not know fear.

I have a dream,
That the hungry will have a feast;
The thirsty will have a well.

I have a dream,
Children will work in a classroom, not in a pit,
They will live a life of love and care
And know no pain.

I have a dream,
That flowers will bloom, animals will breathe in the fresh air
And trees will live,
That is my dream,
There is nothing more to say.

Ruth Taylor (11)
Cardinal Griffin School, Cannock

I Have A Dream

I have a dream that the sun will shine forever,
And I'll grow up to be very, very clever,
I have a dream that all crime will stop,
And that wars will be forgot,
I have a dream that money matters will turn out great,
And everyone will have food on their plate,
I have a dream that all diseases will be gone,
And that my life will go on and on.

Grace Bevan (12)
Cardinal Griffin School, Cannock

I Believe

I believe . . .
In life after death,
And our final last breath,
Of peace spread around,
And no fists are allowed,
Of no sadness in sight,
'Cause you know that's not right!

I believe . . .
Happiness is here,
And it's the end of all fear,
Love has come back,
And happiness is back on track,
That war will never start,
'Cause that's not in our hearts.

I believe . . .
We will all get along,
And that life's as free as songs,
That life's as sweet as cakes,
And we are as peaceful as lakes.
I believe!

Greg Turner (12)
Cardinal Griffin School, Cannock

I Have A Dream

I have a dream that all poverty will end,
I have a dream that animal cruelty will stop,
I have a dream crying children will stop crying,
I have a dream all wars will end,
I have a dream that people will stop murdering other people,
I have a dream everyone will be happy,
I have a dream that the world will be a better place!

Emily Berger (13)
Cardinal Griffin School, Cannock

I Want!

I have a dream of:
World peace,
No guns,
To be what you want to be and
To love each other.

What do you want?
Disease walking around the world,
No sun in the day and
Darkness all around.

If not, say what you want!

I want to learn,
I want a long life,
I want no one to die,
I want no disease.

I want a happy world!

Charlotte Hall (12)
Cardinal Griffin School, Cannock

I Have A Dream

I have a dream . . .
That war will end,
Poverty will be stopped,
And diseases can be cured.

I have a dream . . .
That money will become endless,
Bullying will be punished,
And that everyone will be treated equally.

I have a dream . . .
That nothing will become extinct,
Nothing will be polluted,
And that no one will be judged.

Lauren Elliott (12)
Cardinal Griffin School, Cannock

I Have A Dream

I have a dream that I can make things right,
I have a dream that I can stop the fight,
I have a dream that racism is gone,
I have a dream that the sun shone.

I have a dream that I hope you'll agree,
I have a dream that I'm sure you'll see,
I have a dream that we can live forever,
I have a dream that the trees will stay together.

I have a dream with no world domination,
I have a dream with no extermination,
I have a dream that bullying will go away,
I have a dream that will make you say . . .

I have a dream,
That there is
Peace!

Daniel Hill (11)
Cardinal Griffin School, Cannock

I Have A Dream

What would happen if the money stopped?
If war ended and school went pop?
What would happen if poverty ended?
If the environment and ozone were mended?
What would happen if disease ceased?
If animals came up to us and started to speak?
What would happen to you or me,
If racism and prejudice started to retreat?
Make this world a place for us to stay,
So we can have fun, laugh and play!
This world is the only one we've got!
So look after it, don't let it rot!

Eve Gould (12)
Cardinal Griffin School, Cannock

I Have A Dream

I have a dream,
That everyone's kind,
I have a dream,
That people are never mean,
I have a dream,
That people are great,
I have a dream,
That we live in harmony,
I have a dream,
That will become reality,
I have a dream,
This is my dream,
My dream is that everybody is with everyone
In harmony!

Steven Ravenscroft (12)
Cardinal Griffin School, Cannock

I Have A Dream Of A Long Lasting Life!

I have a dream . . .
Peace, love, laughter, friendship,
What do you want?
No wars, no poverty, no violence, no evil,
I don't want to see,
War, hatred, sadness, loneliness,
I want my world to be happy,
Do you?
I have a dream,
For all to be friends,
For all to be kind,
For all to be respectful of my world, mankind.

Bethany Evans (13)
Cardinal Griffin School, Cannock

I Have A Dream

I have a dream . . .
Fish can swim next to sharks,
That they are happy even in the dark,
That if my heart comes crashing down,
I will promise myself not to frown,
There are no kings and queens to this day,
That war never started, all we do is sit and play,
Cars and buses do not pollute,
Everything is fine at the world's birth,
If people lived just like this,
It would be great because it is my dream,
It is like the world has been swept clean.

Amy Taylor (12)
Cardinal Griffin School, Cannock

I Have A Dream

If you were God looking down on the world,
You would see where I am coming from,
I am coming from a place where we can get food and
Have clothes on our backs,
We have a family and people who love us,
But, I am also coming from a place,
Where we send people off to war,
To fight for us and our country.

Hatred, hurt, humility, death, drugs,
Assault, war, gangs, racial comments.

We can make a difference if we just believe.

Jake Jones (12)
Cardinal Griffin School, Cannock

I Have A Dream

I have a dream of black and white
people holding hands in faith,
I have a dream of war not existing,
I have a dream of everyone having a decent meal each night,
I have a dream that no one is homeless
or in poverty and can get to clean water and medical centres,
I have a dream of people not being in pain,
I have a dream of the world being . . .
Happy,
I want the world to be happy,
Not just me and that is my dream!

Imogen Buck (12)
Cardinal Griffin School, Cannock

I Have A Dream

I have a dream that poverty will end,
I have a dream that broken hearts will mend,
I have a dream that we aren't judged,
I have a dream that my homework isn't smudged,
I have a dream that no one cried,
I have a dream that my grandma never died,
I have a dream that love and compassion are fused,
I have a dream children aren't abused,
I have a dream that disease is gone,
I have a dream that TV standby isn't left on.

Brona Keown (12)
Cardinal Griffin School, Cannock

I Have A Dream

I have a dream that the world will be good,
I have a dream everyone will be happy,
I have a dream everyone will have food,
I have a dream that people will be excited.

I have a dream that all animals will be safe,
I have a dream to stop poverty,
I have a dream the rainforests will stay,
I have a dream fighting will stop.

I have a dream that these dreams will happen.

Liam Robinson (12)
Cardinal Griffin School, Cannock

Dreaming

I had a dream,
That I scored a hat-trick,
And was a rich millionaire.

I had a dream,
That I had a ton of midget gems,
And everything was cheap.

I had a dream,
That dogs didn't poo on the floor,
And football became easier.

Sebastian Sharratt (13)
Cardinal Griffin School, Cannock

I Have A Dream

A dream to stop poverty.
A dream to stop global warming and bullying.
I have a dream,
In my dream there will be no killing, no stealing and no racism.
In my dream,
It will be the perfect world,
There will be raining ice cream,
And an unlimited supply of melted chocolate,
There will also be no school, it will be a perfect world.

David O'Rawe (13)
Cardinal Griffin School, Cannock

My Dream . . .

My dream is that the world will know
That the environment will soon go,
First the trees, then the flowers, *bang, bong!*
Better make the most of them because they'll soon be gone!

Or there is another possibility,
Which is, I hope you will agree,
To get the world to sign a petition,
To save the world on one condition.

This condition is that people will be caring,
Instead of being lazy *and* not sharing.

That they will do some gardening and
Planting, while being jolly and happily chanting . . .

We love the environment,
And we are just brilliant,
And we've done some planting,
Of plants that will,
Bring back the environment
And that's just brill!

Alice Dawson (11)
Cromer High School, Cromer

I Have A Dream

I have a dream,
Of world peace.

I have a dream,
Of children laughing,
And playing without a risk.

I have a dream,
Of flowers growing side by side,
And the sun shining with a smile.

I have a dream
Of world peace.

Jordanna Yeo (12)
Cromer High School, Cromer

My Dad

I have a dream that
I could be my dad,
Because he is funny and awesome.

He treats me well and
He has a beard,
He is very tall and he is a
Prison officer and his name is Jonny.

Jack Newton (11)
Cromer High School, Cromer

Dad

I see dads everywhere,
I feel sad knowing mine's not here,
Scared, worried, now he's not here,
He's a drummer, brick layer, lifeboat man,
His biggest job is being my dad.
I have a dream of seeing him stand there.

Harry Vanzino (11)
Cromer High School, Cromer

World

W onderful
O verpowering
R isky
L ethal
D eathly.

Tom Brodie (12)
Cromer High School, Cromer

My Dream

Slowly my eyes drift closed,
My body pumped by adrenaline,
My mind working my body, getting ready for my hardest move yet,
I turn, my posture perfect,
Then I run and jump, it's over so fast,
I land lightly on my feet having finished my routine,
Suddenly people are cheering and clapping,
Clapping for the girl who has won the Olympics,
I look around, my friends and family are there supporting me,
Their voices louder than anyone's,
Then my eyes snap open,
My dream has ended.

Rhoslyn Roebuck Williams (13)
Dorothy Stringer High School, Brighton

I Have A Dream

I have a dream and I'm not going to be defeated,
This can't go on, I won't let people be mistreated,
I am strong and determined not to stand by,
And let this happen, I have to try.

I have a dream, this cannot go on,
I have a dream, this will not go on.

I have a dream and I'm insistent on winning this war,
We have to stop this, my wounds are sore,
I will win, I will pursue,
This has gone too far, it's untrue.

I have a dream, this cannot go on,
I have a dream, this will not go on.

I have a dream and it's not to be forgotten,
This is so terrible, the behaviour is rotten,
My dream won't be destroyed,
Everybody's lives should be more than enjoyed.

I have a dream, this cannot go on,
I have a dream, this will not go on.

I have a dream, an image in my mind,
With our thoughts and our strong wills combined,
We can make just an image, a faint picture painted in my mind,
Into real life *we* can create a new generation of mankind!

I have a dream this cannot go on,
I have a dream, *we will not let* this go on . . .

Phoebe Dartnell (12)
Dorothy Stringer High School, Brighton

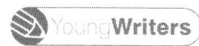

Anne Frank

'I want to go on living after I die',
All Anne thought she was doing
Was keeping a diary,
But she added something,
Something more fiery.

All her thoughts, dreams and emotions,
She poured them all out,
To her listening friend, the diary,
Her secrets it would never shout.

Too near the end of the war,
The eight Jews in hiding were betrayed,
And across nearly each of their paths,
The blackness of death strayed.

Now let this be a warning,
And think of the sheer human force,
As a human race we must make sure,
There is never another Holocaust.

Hannah Clover (12)
Dorothy Stringer High School, Brighton

Sunflower Field

I close my eyes tight,
Wishing to escape cold, dark night,
I take a peek and try to see,
Where on Earth I end up to be,
I look around, smiles peek through,
I'm in sunflower fields with skies of blue,
I walk along and as sun shines bright,
There are people standing for their rights,
The builders are blocked, they cannot pass to destroy
The sunflower field of colour royal,
I join the crowd and the builders retreat,
Let them feel the pain of defeat,
I wake, a happy grin of triumph fastened to my face,
And imagine the sunflower field of peace and grace.

Miranda Streames (12)
Dorothy Stringer High School, Brighton

I Have A Dream

Life is a gift given to us,
To choose what we want, what we want to say,
Life is for giving, not taking away.

War is a plague given to us,
A shot from a gun,
A stab in the night,
A war can't be won,
There's no victory in a fight.

Is this what we want?
Is this what we choose?
To do with our lives, our only chance,
We are but one move in a much bigger dance.

For war cannot win,
Hope will live on,
And the more we hope,
The more it urges us on.

To be done with the pain,
And the tears and the strife,
That battle can bring into a man's life.

But one man is just one,
But two is one more,
And a whole world together,
Could drive out the war.

But we'll need every man,
To bring us that dove,
Of a life of prosperity,
Of happiness and love.

Life will out.

Ellen Lawrence-Clery (11)
Farlingaye High School, Woodbridge

Stand For What You Believe In

Stand for what you believe in,
Don't let anyone change your mind,
You are your own person,
Believe in yourself,
The soul is a very powerful thing.

All of us should make our own mind up,
And not change because of anyone,
Don't let anyone push you down,
So they can be mighty,
Stand your ground and mind,
No matter what.

It's kind of like war,
People maybe don't want to fight,
But they are made to,
So stand your ground and mind,
No matter what.

Some people in life,
Will want to be the bigger person,
But you know better,
You are strong,
The soul is a very powerful thing.

People everywhere on this Earth,
Are forced to do things,
And they can't stand up for what they believe in,
So be strong, powerful and be yourself,
Stand up for what *you* believe in.

Being backed into a corner,
Hearts beating like a roller coaster,
Someone whispering in your ear,
But you're saying, 'No!'
You are standing up for what you believe in.

Sophie Fry (13)
Grainville School, Jersey

All You Have To Say Is, 'No!'

Drifting, drifting to the land of nothing,
You're seeing stars, see a penguin frothing,
Your head is spinning round and round,
You're falling, slipping, to the ground.

All that you have to say is, 'No!'
And all this emptiness soon will go.

You're skipping around,
Round the high street shops,
The cars all beep,
But you never stop.

Think you're invincible,
And that you can fly,
But you will soon fall unconscious,
And will most likely die.

There's many ways to take your crack,
In your arm and round the back,
But your face will drop on each side,
Is it worth it, this merciful ride?

All that you have to say is, 'No!'
And all this emptiness soon will go.

You won't be loved,
And you won't be liked,
For evermore,
A frightful sight.

All that you have to say is, 'No!'
And all this emptiness soon will go.

So stop this nonsense,
Restart your brain,
And hopefully your life,
Will be on track again.

Go get some help,
Call that magical number,
Or visit the website,
Don't be a cucumber.

All that you have to say is, 'No!'
And all this emptiness soon will go.

Ossia O'Donovan (13)
Grainville School, Jersey

What Do You Believe In?

What do you believe in?
What is your soul's desire?
Can it change the world?
So spread the word,
For it might change the world.

No matter what people think,
Your ideas are important,
So spread the word,
For it may change the world.

Stand up for what you believe in,
For it may change the world for generations ahead,
For your opinion is important,
So spread the word,
For it may change the world.

No matter what people think,
Your ideas are important,
So spread the word,
For it may change the world.

So if you have something important to say,
Speak your mind,
For it is important,
So spread the word,
For it may change the world.

Christopher Aubert (13)
Grainville School, Jersey

It's Up To You!

Stand up for what you believe in,
Don't let your dream go,
Everyone should respect you,
So let the people know,
It's up to you.

Why is it always violence,
Going on around us?
It doesn't solve anything,
No one needs to make a fuss,
It's up to you.

Stand up for what you believe in,
Don't let your dream go,
Everyone should respect you,
So let the people know,
It's up to you.

Fun, happiness and peace,
Is what the world's about,
Live each day like you're dying the next,
Come on everybody, scream and shout,
It's up to you.

Stand up for what you believe in,
Don't let your dream go,
Everyone should respect you,
So let the people know,
It's up to you.

Friendship and love,
Why can't there be more of this
Instead of war and violence?
It's not hard to miss,
It's up to you!

Sophie Rolland (12)
Grainville School, Jersey

Why?

When the black children were told they were
Different from all the rest,
That they couldn't go to school
With the white children,
That they could never be best.

They were told they could never achieve,
Never be president or king,
All their hopes disappeared,
And they were left with nothing.

They had no rights, no ability to speak,
They were separated from the rest of the world
And their future looked bleak.

They were treated like animals,
Hated by white people, then Nelson Mandela
Came and they all saw the light.

He told them there was hope and to never give up,
We will all be the same one day,
If only we could trust.

Slowly things are changing,
As people begin to see, that there really is no difference
Between you and me,
So forget about the outside and think about the in,
Then we will all join together and
That way we all win!

Shannon Hearne (12)
Grainville School, Jersey

This Is What I Want

I have my ideas to what I want in the future,
What I want, I need to try my hardest,
I want to be a lawyer, help those that are innocent,
This is what I want . . .

I also want to help animals,
Save them from danger,
I want to save them from dying and also crying,
This is what I want . . .

I want to be a lifeguard,
Swim through many oceans,
Save the people in danger before they get hurt,
This is what I want . . .

I want to see people smile,
Smile with joy, not sadness,
I want to help them not be sad,
This is what I want . . .

I want to help those in need,
The ones that need more than us,
The ones that have nothing and need someone to trust,
This is what I want.

Carla De Freitas
Grainville School, Jersey

I Wished

I wished upon a star,
And my wish came true,
Because of that I travelled far,
So can you!

I wished upon a star,
And I had fun,
Even if it was bizarre,
I connected with everyone.

I wished upon a star,
And my wish came true,
It was to be a dancer,
What about you?

I wished upon a star,
And my wish came true,
But that just shows,
What wishing on stars can do!

I wished upon a star,
Now I'm no longer blue,
I have gone very far,
That's what you could do!

Katie Fox (13)
Grainville School, Jersey

Respect Your Parents

Think, just think when you're annoyed with
Your mum or dad,
The way they are good to you but you don't approve,
But think, they care for you,
Gave you ice creams when you were small,
So do them a favour and give them a bit more respect.

Think, just think how they brought you up,
Gave you a roof over your head,
Helped with your homework,
Sent you to school even if you didn't want to,
So you would get a good education,
When you were ill and sat on your sofa,
With a blanket watching your favourite TV programme,
So just respect them.

Think, just think when you're getting bullied at school,
And you tell them they can make it stop,
They give you presents at Christmas,
Even the latest games console,
But don't be ashamed if you didn't get what you wanted,
At least they tried.

Curtis Monks (12)
Grainville School, Jersey

Just Say, 'No'

Just say, 'No,'
To people that offer you bad things.

Just say, 'No,'
To peer pressure.

Just say, 'No,'
To bullying.

Just say, 'No,'
To fatty foods.

And say, 'Yes,'
To your dreams.

Say, 'Yes,'
To your rights.

And say what you have to say,
And do what you want to do.

Pedro De Abreu (13)
Grainville School, Jersey

Untitled

My dream,
Is to help others achieve their long life dream,
My dream,
Is to care for the less fortunate people,
My dream,
Is to ban racism,
My dream,
Is to have a good life,
My dream,
Is to teach other members of our world education
To be successful in their lives,
My dream,
Is to just practise, practise, practise.

Michael Fisher
Grainville School, Jersey

What If . . .

The smile you once saw was gone forever,
And the frequent laugh you heard was shot?
The features of your dearest face was gone,
Dead, down forever?

What if . . .
The growing nation cries and weeps of despair,
Of the loved one, that we do care?
But if we all work together as one,
No matter where we are from.

What if . . .
Winston Churchill did give up?
Then we would not be the nation we are today,
Put our shoulders back and stand proud,
To get our loved ones out.

What if . . .
We got the soldiers out of Iraq,
And they could have the Sunday roast with their family?
We would hear them laugh again,
And relight the candle that went out.

What if . . .
We could all make a difference,
And change the world to one community,
Bring the soldiers out the war,
And fight for what we belleve in?

Talluah Brewer
Grainville School, Jerrsey

I Have A Dream

I have a dream dat,
I have a dream dat,
I have a dream dat dere woz no illness,
No one would starve,
We would all live together.

I have a dream dat,
I have a dream dat,
I have a dream that dere woz no racism in our lives,
Fink bt it, we're all equal.

I have a dream dat,
I have a dream dat,
I have a dream dat all lives should be fun,
Everybody could live life to da max,
After they've hoovered up wiv dere Vax.

I have a dream dat,
I have a dream dat,
I have a dream dat dere woz no scaries on da streets,
So shuv it!

I have a dream dat,
I have a dream dat,
I have a dream dat dere woz no child abuse,
Lives wouldn't be da same,
Cos dere would be no crime.

I have a dream,
Well actually,
I ain't fakin',
I ain't fakin',
I ain't fakin' dis,
I aint' fakin,
I ain't fakin,
Do suttin bt it.

Hannah Baldwin (12)
Harris Middle School, Lowestoft

I Have A Dream

No more muggin',
No more violence,
Hunger stops,
Homes saved,
Instead of no homes,
New ones are made,
That's my dream.

Reduce diseases,
Make clean water,
Save sons,
And save daughters,
That's what I believe,
I have a dream.

Everyone's the same,
Don't be treated differently,
Don't be stuck at home,
Cos people are in pain,
That's my dream to save them.

People dead,
No longer with us,
You'd be upset,
So use your head,
That's my dream.

No more poverty,
Being all poor,
Don't cover yourself with no door,
That's my dream.

People are unhappy,
We want everything,
All right now,
So don't wave around and be all clappy,
That's my dream.

God made children not to be abused,
Don't make them slum around,
All battered and bruised,
That's my dream.

Dreams are dreams,
Not always true,
Hopefully this one,
Has gone through to you,
Make this your dream!

Zara Anderson & Shannon Lowe (10)
Harris Middle School, Lowestoft

I Have A Dream

I have a dream that we can all be free,
With happiness and laughter and all live happily ever after.

I have a dream that the world will be a happy place,
No thick or thin, bad or good
Just all my love for the peeps in ma hood.

I have a dream that animals can be free,
Instead of being in captivity,
In the wild, they have fun
But I don't think they'll like it
If they are in your tum!

I have a dream that the economic crisis will be solved
And in years to come it will be old news, *hola!*

Right, polar bears die because you're throwing your KitKat wrapper on the floor.
Now pick it up you silly fool!

I have a dream that there are no scary peeps on the street
Taking us in and giving us a beat.

I have a dream that bullying will be in da past
Just because of your cast.

I have a dream that we can all get along,
That's why we're singing this song.

I have a dream that the kids in Africa
Will get their lives back and get a nice snack!

Chanelle Woods (12), Charlotte Augood & Daisy Gyapong (11)
Harris Middle School, Lowestoft

I Have A Dream

I have a dream to write
I could do it all night.
My imagination runs wild,
Feel like an everlasting child.

I have a dream that dragons will evolve again.
They'll fly higher than Big Ben
They can go all over the sphere.
And the whole world will love to hear.

I have a dream to write an amazing story
So it can be told on CBBC Jackanory.
We can stay young forever like in Never Never Land
That would be grand.

I have a dream that all the money I earn
I will get a rescue horse, give it loads of love
Help it to learn,
I will give it everything needed with care
Get the right supplements to make it have healthy horse hair.

I have a dream to form a band
In a parallel land
We will be so out there
Won't be on front page magazine called Stare.

I have a dream that all the animal abuse stops
And that one day the level drops,
And we can care about our pets
Instead of sending them dead to the vets.

I have a dream that there's no more bloodshed
Over colour and we can all sit together and drink a Bud.
To care for every race, to make it a better place.

Lola Matthews (12)
Harris Middle School, Lowestoft

I Have A Dream

I have a dream that no more people in the world will be poor
I hope that there is no more war

I have a dream that there will be no more hunger
No one does diseases, no one does death
I'm afraid there is no more food left

I have a dream for lots more breath
For taking people's breath away, people's death

I have a dream for no more litter
All the food is going quicker

I have a dream for much more food
For people to eat and enjoy

I have a dream for no more devastation
I have a dream for more fun and play

Why should humans not have a good time?
Take notice of this rhyme and *help!*

I have a dream, what is yours?
Another bad day for a lot of poor people
Please come and help by giving up your pay.

Lots of dreams do come true
So why don't you have this dream too?

Come and save the children
Make them have some fun
If they are hungry, give them a bun

Please come and help
Some kids yelp, some are in pain
Make it rain.

Shannon Lockwood (12)
Harris Middle School, Lowestoft

I Have A Dream

I have a dream for no more war
No more people living poor
That is my dream, what is yours?
Remember this rap for evermore.

I have a dream for no more death
No more taking people's breath
That is my dream, what is yours?
Remember this rap for evermore.

I have a dream for no more hunger
People's lives get lived longer
That is my dream, what is yours?
Remember this rap for evermore.

I have a dream for black and white
To sleep together peacefully at night
That is my dream, what is yours?
Remember this rap for evermore.

I have a dream for no more pain
No more playing silly games
That is my dream, what is yours?
Remember this rap for evermore.

Why, why, why should people cry
'Cause other people are being sly?
That is my dream, what is yours?
Remember this rap for evermore.

Why should people not be happy?
We're all different so don't be snappy.

Lucy Patterson & Rebecca Foster (12)
Harris Middle School, Lowestoft

I Have A Dream

I have a dream that children will not suffer
'Cause we will make them tougher
I have a dream everyone is free
They have dreams like you and me.

Help them now please, oh please
Don't make them get down and beg on their knees
Don't let them get whipped on their backs
They're not different because they're black.

Poor people should have a life like us
Or at least one where they can pay for a bus
If you've got money give, give, give
Let the poor people live, live, live.

They live on the streets, they don't have homes
This is why they beg and this is why they moan
The end is what it's all about
That's the bit where you scream and shout.

People out there, put your hands in the air
Give us a shout if you really do care
If you have a dream the same as this song
Don't let this go on and on.

Charmaine Allen (11), Neive Banellis & Sophie Bunn (12)
Harris Middle School, Lowestoft

I Have A Dream

I have a dream that all the wars will end.
I have a dream that black and white both have rights.
I have a dream that black and white will live in harmony.
I have a dream that no more crime will be committed.
I have a dream that the world will learn to stop being racist.
I have a dream that the world will be in peace again.

James Hedges (12)
Harris Middle School, Lowestoft

I Have A Dream

I have a dream, make it happy
I have a dream, make it snappy
I have a dream that children will
Have food to be able to eat their fill
That will give them a thrill.

I have a dream that everybody will have money
Then maybe their lives will be funny
I have a dream everybody can have a tree
And all the animals will be as free
As they could want to be.

I have a dream that you can walk down the street
And don't have to worry about who you're going to meet
I have a dream that everybody can see what they want to see
I have a dream that people will be around to see their child's baby.

I have a dream that just maybe
All of us can have a Wii or a PSP
I have a dream that nobody will scream in fright
That they might be stabbed
I have a dream that the world will be happy
I have a dream.

Harry Lawrence & Luke Gault (12)
Harris Middle School, Lowestoft

I Have A Dream

I have a dream we're so keen
To stop *pollution* know what I mean?

I have a dream you gotta lean
To help prevent dis horrible scene, *global warming*.

I have a dream use a gene
Poverty it's just plain mean.

I have a dream use a jumpin' bean
Av u seen the mean *crime?*

I have a dream, don't be so mean
You gotta clean up dis scene, *child abuse.*

I have a dream the world oughta be clean
Know what you've seen, life's so mean, *illnesses.*

I have a dream, are you a teen
Who is mean?
You gotta be seen right on screen, bang out *bullying.*

I have a dream no litter-reeing
People should gleam, we're a team
So keep it clean, *littering is mean.*

Alice Cheverton (12) & Becky Durrant (11)
Harris Middle School, Lowestoft

I Have A Dream

I have a dream there is no war
I have a dream that there will be more money for the poor

I have a dream we will all smile
I have a dream life will be less vile

I have a dream black people will be allowed
I have a dream they will be astounded

I have a dream for no more global warming
I have a dream they will give me a warning

I have a dream no one will be sad
I have a dream no one will be mad

I have a dream this world will change
I have a dream that money will be exchanged

I have a dream that Martin Luther King is not dead
I have a dream that everyone will be fed

I have a dream that everyone's wealthy
I have a dream everyone's healthy.

Ben Cook (11), Darius Mullen & Joshua Thorpe (12)
Harris Middle School, Lowestoft

I Have A Dream

I have a dream that the world isn't mean
And all the children in African are healthy and clean.

I have a dream that poor children can be seen
Because they need to keep their hygiene.

I have a dream that young children can be seen
On roads without the sunbeam.

I have a dream that the world has no violence
And is keen.

I have a dream that we will all take this in, to note.

Nicholas Harrison (11)
Harris Middle School, Lowestoft

I Have A Dream

I have a dream, that one day
The Afghani war will stop. Yeah.

I have a dream, that one day
The perverts will not exist. Yeah.

I have a dream, that one day
We'll all be able to live together. Yeah.

I have a dream, that one day
Pollution will stop for good. Yeah.

I have a dream, that one day
South Korea will stop creating bombs. Yeah.

I have a dream, that one day
Religion will all make sense. Yeah.

I have a dream, that one day
The rainforest won't be cut down. Yeah.

I have a dream, that one day
The world will be a better place. Yeah.

Lewis Connolly, Elliot Waters & Paul Tully (12)
Harris Middle School, Lowestoft

I Have A Dream

I have a dream, that we can make the world a better place.
I have a dream, that there's not gonna be any violence in this world.
I have a dream, that we're gonna close the door on poverty.
I have a dream, that children will not starve any longer.
I have a dream, that we're gonna make the people smile happily.
I have a dream, that everyone will have what they deserve.
I have a dream, that we can stop global warming.
I have a dream, that we can help wildlife.
We have a dream of freedom;
Let's put it forward to succeed.

Michael Mullender (12) & Kim Smith (11)
Harris Middle School, Lowestoft

I Have A Dream

I have a dream, that one day none of the kids will go hungry in another country
My dream is to
My dream is to
My dream is to make the world a better place
To make the world a better place to live.

I have a dream, that one day all the kids can run free, in their own little way
My dream is to
My dream is to
My dream is to make the world a better place
To make the world a better place to live.

I have a dream, that one day no kids will get abused by their parents
My dream is to
My dream is to
My dream is to make the world a better place
To make the world a better place to live.

Kelsie Cressy (12) & Lucy Brooks (11)
Harris Middle School, Lowestoft

I Have A Dream!

I have a dream, that black and white kids of the world
Can walk hand in hand down non-racist streets

I have a dream, that black and white men and women
Have the same rights as everyone else

I have a dream, that we aren't judged by the colour of our skin
But by the heart inside us.

I have a dream, that one day the world
With black and white people will come to live in peace

I have a dream, that black and white people
Depending on their religions
Will be able to share special occasions with each other.

Jack Morgan (12)
Harris Middle School, Lowestoft

I Have A Dream

I have a dream that all good people can live
Swept into a happy life, democracy rules.

I have a dream that war will come to an end
Shouting no longer, come and join the peace conga.

I have a dream that sweet harmony is among us
Without peace the world will come to an end.

I have a dream that hostages get released
Peace, peace and cease the wars.

I have a dream that among us
He rises again, come and join the peace conga.

I have a dream that peace will settle in the world
And we can all live in sweet harmony.

I have a dream that black people will be set free forever
I have a dream.

Cameron Moore, Danny Cook & Liam Bowen (12)
Harris Middle School, Lowestoft

I Have A Dream

I have a dream that everyone can walk hand in hand . . . whatever religion.
I have a dream that everyone's equal
And that war will end, showing peace, not hatred.
I have a dream that everyone isn't judged by their skin
But by the heart inside of them.
I have a dream that everyone can have equal food, money and clean water.
I have a dream that children get the right education.
Shelter, food and clothing to survive.
I have a dream that male and female can be together
With no problems and no fighting occurring.
I have a dream that every man and woman has the same rights.
I have a dream that together we can make this dream a reality.

Josie McWade & Bethaney Picton (12)
Harris Middle School, Lowestoft

I Have A Dream

I have a dream
That one day global warming will disappear.

I have a dream
The rainforests will regrow.

I have a dream
The tigers will repopulate.

I have a dream
All extinct animals will become unextinct.

I have a dream
War in all countries will cease.

I have a dream
All poor get the riches they require.

I have a dream
The world will be in harmony.

Sam McMillan (11)
Harris Middle School, Lowestoft

I Have A Dream

I have a dream that people won't be poor
I have a dream that their cuts aren't sore
I have a dream that they have homes
I have a dream that they have hair combs
I have a dream that they have food
I have a dream that people aren't crude
I have a dream that there's no gun crime
I have a dream that criminals do the time
I have a dream to stop racism
I have a dream that they go to prison
I have a dream!

Deryn Corbett & Phoebe McCann (12)
Harris Middle School, Lowestoft

I Have A Dream!

I have a dream,
That when you walk down the street
You won't have to worry about who you're gonna meet.

Whether you'll get shot,
Because in this hood,
The amount of gangs is increasing more and more every day.
Drugs are being dealt and now I'm knelt
On one knee praying that they'll see . . .

Because I have a dream,
That scientists will see,
Animal testing is not the way to be,
Think about all the ones that are going,
Insects, polar bears, tigers and many others

Do you have a dream?

Shannon Anderson & Ellie Le Grice (12)
Harris Middle School, Lowestoft

I Have A Dream

I have a dream, that everyone will be treated the same,
I have a dream, that no more people will be ill,
I have a dream, that magic is real,
I have a dream, that everyone will have a happy life,
I have a dream, that there will be no more violence and killing for no reason,
I have a dream, that every child will have a family,
I have a dream, that we won't have to kill living things just for food,
I have a dream, that everyone will have a proper home,
I have a dream, that this world can be a happy place.
I have a dream!

Ebony Theaker & Kailey Hugman (12)
Harris Middle School, Lowestoft

I Have A Dream . . .

Of a new horizon, a clear night
A baffling tongue, a candle instead of a light
Buzzing markets, dusty ground
A tropical morning, an exotic sound

Of fresh spices with their enveloping smells
Eye-grabbing colours, pealing bells
Pitch-black ravines, people selling their wares
Other worldly fruits and prickly pears

Of colossal palm trees, a milky coconut
A golden beach, a bamboo beach hut
A vast stretch of sea, a coral reef
A ferocious tiger with pearlescent teeth

Of mosaic ceilings, tiled floors
Tapestry embossed walls with wood-carved doors
Tessellated patterns, kaleidoscope shapes
An alien world which is my escape

Of a rainforest umbrella that shelters me from a monsoon
The burst of freshness that follows and radiant flowers that still bloom
Luscious trees and plants - the world's best perfumery
Their petals a whirl of Mother Nature's intricate embroidery

Of a rickety bridge, over a roaring river
And breezes that refuse to make you shiver
Rolling hills, entertained by a choir of birds
So much beauty that I am lost for words

Of a ball of fire that is the sun
A cornflower-blue sky that makes the clouds run
Humid temperatures which chase away rain
A lifetime of peacefulness, daisy chains

Of a ride on an elephant, a stampede through a jungle
Sari-wrapped people, their world at a different angle
A cluster of cosy little mud huts with straw for their rugs
A well to be my source of water which bare hands have dug . . .

But now my palm tree is a lamp post, my roaring river a road
My mosaic wall graffiti - I'm back to realistic mode
My choir of birds a tacky pop song, my strange breeze a gale

My idealistic forecast is ruined by hail

Baffling languages make way for slang
My sari-wrapped people become a vicious gang
My clear night is interrupted by skyscrapers
My lifetime of peacefulness is contradicted by the papers

My cluster of cosy mud huts are sludgy puddles on the ground
My pealing bells, don't even make their sound
My vast stretch of sea becomes a vast stretch of grey
The sun won't shine, not even in May

My cornflower-blue sky is a polluted mess
My calm frame of mind is engulfed by stress
My elephant transport is a bus where you have to pay
My exquisite-smelling spices are barged out of the way

My world is back to normal - normal is back to my world
But as logic takes my mind once more (after it had leapt, bound and twirled)
I glimpse those golden beaches and pitch-black ravines
And, unfortunately, they must remain in my dreams.

Molly Padgham Hugh (13)
Helenswood Lower School, St Leonards on Sea

I Have A Dream

I have a dream
My dream is . . .
To stop the world from being evil
But I'm too feeble.

I have a dream
My dream is . . .
To love the world as it is
As well as my little sis.

I have a dream
My dream is . . .
To make the world a better place
For love not war, a place of peace.

Shannon Hutchinson (12)
Helenswood Lower School, St Leonards on Sea

A Thousand Splendid Dreams

I will gaze upon the towers,
Each spire coated in sparkling dust,
Golden in the fantastic sun,
The sky streaked in an exotic,
Array of warming colours,
Smeared with clear water from
The depths of the Venetian ocean,
I will sail in wooden boats,
Past mangroves tall,
Their roots supple and
Strong
Strong, as the words, which
I will write upon a piece of empty paper
High on a hill, stretching afar, an iridescent sea,
Which
Will lie beneath my poems
My stories,
Fast-forming, swirling, touching
Everyone who reads,
Who breathes,
Who understands,
Who believes
There's more to life than
Winning,
More complex than fighting,
With useless weapons, glinting from a broken sun
And
There are more layers to a dream than
Imaginable
For these are my dreams
Which
I will scatter
Weightless as lavender upon my pillow,
As I sleep.

Pasha Milburn (13)
Helenswood Lower School, St Leonards on Sea

My Dream

They have a dream to change the world,
To erase poverty, crime and war,
Maybe I want all this,
But who says I'm one of them?
I have a dream
To give people better lives,
Regardless of where they come from
Or what they look like,
I too, have a dream.
Yes, I will have to aim high,
Climb every mountain, swim every sea,
However, it is for anyone and everyone
To be wherever they want to be.
I have a dream
To help the underprivileged
To solve problems and to find solutions,
Sort out worries and bottled up issues,
I can dig deep enough
Because I have a dream.
Dreams come in all sorts of shapes and sizes,
But they are all possible to achieve
If you try whole-heartedly,
If you are confident, if you believe.
I have a dream
To cross out the hurt
Caused by unnecessary anger,
To overcome fears, to wipe away tears,
I have decided, that is my dream.

Isra Husain (13)
Helenswood Lower School, St Leonards on Sea

I Have A Dream

I have a dream,
That destructive bombs will reverse back into the war planes,
That violent flooding water will suck back into the drains.

I wish,
That all the innocent sufferers will be reborn,
That life's book will not be torn.

What if,
World peace comes tomorrow,
To block out thieves and times of sorrow?

I think,
That tears should be cries of joy,
And cruel remarks should not destroy.

Maybe one day,
All human rights will be respected,
And global warming stops, the Earth will be protected.

Would it be possible,
For the world to live forever,
And people believe and never say never?

I have a dream,
That the only world domination is world peace.

Jessica Bartlett (13)
Helenswood Lower School, St Leonards on Sea

A Place

Think of a place with nullified shouting
We admire a place with peace in the world
For all those at war fighting for us
Or an ambition for everyone
Or even a place with obtained confidence
And no violence
A place for all to be free.

Laura Kent (11)
Helenswood Lower School, St Leonards on Sea

Tame Fire

What's wrong with this planet?
I stand here and ask of you that
And what happened to
Those years long ago
Before Man's invention, tame fire?

And where now is the free land
The field where all may grow?
Cut and burned and formed, I say
That's where your blessed field's gone.

And why, I ask
Is God a man?
What's wrong with fur and feathers?
Would Man God say chop
The beloved trees?
Well yes, it seems He would.

I have a dream
It's simple and good
For Man to become his shadow
For Man to sulk back
To dark fur and trees
And forget the taming of fire.

Samantha Sebbage (14)
Helenswood Lower School, St Leonards on Sea

Homeless

Another horrid day,
As I walked along the streets,
I peered down to the floor,
And saw my bloody feet.

I carried on going,
Although I was in pain,
I couldn't wait for my food,
My one and only grain.

I played on my guitar,
As generous people gave,
I would use the money to feed my dog,
And leftovers I would save.

I wish I had a house,
Where I could sleep in a cosy bed,
A warm and safe environment,
With a roof upon my head.

But for now it's a cardboard box,
Where I get wetter and wetter,
For I am a homeless man,
Oh, I wish I could get better.

Bethan Willard (13)
Helenswood Lower School, St Leonards on Sea

I Have A Dream

I have a dream,
That some day we will see what war has done to our world,
We will stop,
We will see.

I have a dream,
That the hatred war creates will stop
And we can rewind to a time when we lived in a haven of happiness,
We will stop,
We will see.

I have a dream,
That our political leaders will shake hands
And see that we are all equal,
We will stop,
We will see.

But my biggest dream,
Is that my generation and generations to come
Will see a world drained of hatred and hurt
A world where everyone can live in peace,
We *can* stop,
We *can* see.

Maddie Thomson (13)
Helenswood Lower School, St Leonards on Sea

The Space Above

Birds swoop gracefully around its heavens,
They take off from the peaceful shores.
The vast amounts of space above,
Untouched by human claws.

Great white mammoths,
Float in mid-air.
Cruising the soft winds,
Streaks of gold peek through their hair.

Glistening drops of melted diamonds,
Untouched, undamaged until they drop.
Delicate butterflies pondering the skies,
Soft silk petals are where they stop.

Birds swoop gracefully around its heavens,
They take off from the peaceful shores.
The vast amounts of space above,
Untouched by human claws.

Jazmin Pook (13)
Helenswood Lower School, St Leonards on Sea

Writing Eyes

When I write through my hands
I write through my eyes
I put things in a way
To make you realise

When I write through my mind
The whole world is crying
Some with joy
But some are slowly dying

When I write through my dreams
The world's a better place
No crying or poverty
I let my pencil race

When I write through my heart
I try and make you see
The world can be a peaceful place
If you let your dreams run free.

Kathleen Stevenson (14)
Helenswood Lower School, St Leonards on Sea

I Have A Dream

I have a dream of happiness
Where the golden land is joined by silver bridges
Made of words

The people use paper to communicate, inspire and live
They wear what they are proudly and attractively

The rain is beautiful, the wind sings sweetly
And the sun is amazing

Where I have a desk, a small photo of my son
My love imprinted on my heart
And a smile on my face

I have a dream of happiness
Still curious about the secrets
But so calm, so right, so home.

Georgina Browning (14)
Helenswood Lower School, St Leonards on Sea

I Have A Dream

I have a dream that I will be free
Free from the cloud that hangs over me
Free to be anything I want to be
Not to pretend for any of my friends.

I have a dream that I will not be teased
Not be teased about my family, please
Or teased about the colour of my skin
I'd rather be my colour than pale and thin.

I am not a toy to be played with
Pushed or pulled or bullied to amuse
All I dream is for you to accept me
For who I really can be.

Emma Browning (12)
Helenswood Lower School, St Leonards on Sea

I Have A Dream

M ake me into a vampire
Y oung vampires are cute

D rink our blood and
R un away
E ven though I'm scary
A nd terrifying
M aybe we can be friends.

Lara Young (11)
Mayfield School, Chorley

I Have A Dream

M y dream about being a pop star
Y ou could hear me singing

D ancing on the stage
R ich pop stars
E very hour pop stars sing
A ll the time
M aking people happy.

Ashley Hinds (12)
Mayfield School, Chorley

My Dream

M y dream is
Y orkie my horse

D ark chocolate colour
R iding on horses
E xciting
A nd fast
M y horse is fantastic.

Jessyca Unsworth (12)
Mayfield School, Chorley

I Have A Dream

M aking things to eat
Y oghurt is the best

D ancing down the kitchen
R ed jelly and ice cream
E gg scrambled
A pple crumble and custard
M edal for my cooking.

Natasha Lee (11)
Mayfield School, Chorley

My Dream

M agic
Y ellow submarine

D reaming in bed
R acing driver
E ating at the café
A lways playing football
M aking music.

Mark Hinds (16)
Mayfield School, Chorley

My Dream

M aking ice cream
Y ummy in my tummy

D elicious to eat
R eally delicious
E very different flavour
A pple and strawberry
M ixing up the cream.

Catherine Reece (12)
Mayfield School, Chorley

I Have A Dream

M y dream is to be in High School Musical
Y ou could see me singing

D ancing to the music
R unning to the lockers
E veryone having fun
A game of basketball
M aking lots of friends.

Kimberley Smith (12)
Mayfield School, Chorley

I Have A Dream

M y computer game
Y ou have to race

D angerous
R acing for the torches
E xciting
A lways win
M usic.

Christopher Macdonald (13)
Mayfield School, Chorley

I Have A Dream

I have a dream that:
There will be no more wars
We recycle more
Animal cruelty stops
We use eco-friendly cars
We will produce less carbon emissions
We use less plastic
That is my dream.

Laura Colebrooke (13)
Penryn College, Penryn

Imagine

Imagine
A world without conflict

Imagine
A clean planet

Imagine
No sadness

Imagine
A happy ever after

Imagine
A world where evil was punished

Imagine
A world without evil

Imagine
No pain

Imagine
Immortality

Imagine
Time and space were under control

Imagine
Safety

Imagine
Freedom

Imagine
How boring it would be.

Mark Ryan (12)
Penryn College, Penryn

I Have A Dream

Imagine
A world without dispute
Imagine
A place with no wars
Imagine
An ocean drained of all oil
Imagine
A sky with no smoke
Imagine
A forest rich in green
Imagine
The trees in bloom
Imagine
The ice caps looming tall
Imagine
The sea down low
Imagine
A voice amongst the crowd
Imagine
A cry for help
Imagine
A word to change the world
Imagine
A single hope
Imagine.

Molly Johnstone-Clark (12)
Penryn College, Penryn

Martin Luther King

Against every single odd
One man stood up for his rights
And changed the world.

Kai Blackmore (13)
Penryn College, Penryn

Imagine You Could Have One Wish . . .

Imagine you could have one wish
A wish that could change the world
A wish that could change how people think.

Would you stop war and create world peace?
Or would it be smaller
One that would help someone close to you?

Would your wish help someone create their goal and achieve?
Or would your wish be a small gesture
Make someone smile and laugh?

Would your wish make someone's dream come true and make them warm inside?
Or would your wish help someone's self-confidence
And make them believe in themselves?

Would your wish help someone who is on the sidelines
Be a part of something and help them belong?
Or would your wish help someone beat bullying
And help them go forward?

Imagine if your wish would inspire someone
Make them have one wish, a wish that could change the world
A wish that could change how people think.

Yzobel Wilkinson (13)
Penryn College, Penryn

I Have A Dream

I have a dream that Cornwall will be green.
The trees will stand tall like the cathedral St Paul.
The beaches will gleam like the big sunbeam.
Cornwall will be strong and last for ever so long.
The views of Pendennis Castle don't compare to the cattle.
Cornwall will last for evermore, so please don't close the door.

Michael Snell & Alex Skelton (13)
Penryn College, Penryn

I Have A Dream

Imagine
You are the person who rules the world
Imagine
All people are treated as equals
Imagine
A life without murder
Imagine
A life without bullies
Imagine
A life full of peace and happiness
Imagine
A life where everyone has a say in what goes on in the world
Imagine
A life where everyone is rich and powerful
Imagine
A life without the police
Imagine
A life without suicide
Imagine
A life without telly
Imagine
A life where you're the only human in existence.

Connor Clements (14)
Penryn College, Penryn

Smile!

Smile!
Like you've never smiled before,
Make it touch your ears,
Give someone a great big grin.

Smile!
And the world will smile back,
Let the happiness fill you up,
Let the joy burst out.

Smile!
Let someone know you're there for them,
Cheer them up,
Make them believe in their dreams.

Smile!
Like you've never smiled before,
Make it touch your ears,
Give someone a great big grin.

Smile!

Bethany Wilkinson (12)
Penryn College, Penryn

Never Give Up

Don't ever give up,
Keep trying to reach your goals.
Try to chase your dreams.
The eight time Olympic gold medallist
Michael Phelps never gave up.
Always attempting,
Like a shark in the water,
Never relenting.

Kieran Pooley (12)
Penryn College, Penryn

Jet Li - Never Give Up

Imagine being Jet Li
You will be totally fearless
A hero without equal
A Wushu master
He has trained all his life
And has become so unique
Now he has a great job
He cannot ask for more
The films he has made
Will be remembered for a long time
In China he is like a god
Strong, bold and powerful
A 15 time gold medallist
In the Chinese Olympics
Jet Li inspires me
Because he never gives up
And now I realise there is more to life
Than quitting when the going gets tough.

Sam Julian (12)
Penryn College, Penryn

I Have A Dream

I have a dream that one day there will be an end to poverty.
That men, women and children won't roam the streets
With ragged clothes begging for just a little of your meal,
Your money or your kindness to spare them just enough
To give strength to them in a way
Which will fill them not to the extent
Where they become full, but just slightly
To give them the least of energy
To continue their journey of begging
In which they endeavour.

In this dream both eligible, prestigious and fortunate
Are equal with the less fortunate.
The fortunate will care for and share
With the less fortunate
And they will live in a loving society
While showing empathy towards one another.

The unfortunate will not be ignored or pushed aside
But they are responsible for the fortunate.
This dream shows the global community improved
And helps this world be a better and safer environment
To live in for us and our future generations.

If only we could love each other, be thoughtful,
Show respect, be kind and be supportive,
This would be an achievement
We all would be successful In achieving.

Angela Liu (16)
Port Moresby International School, Papua New Guinea

The Dream Of A Better Place

To have a dream of hope is something rare, yet
For peace on Earth and endless joy, if only this was the deal
No sorrow, no suffering
No hurting and no crying
If only tears of sadness became tears of sheer bliss . . .

Where the wars erupted from the inner suburbs
To the country as a whole
It would turn into an eruption of peace
Where hunger at its worst and poverty to the extreme
Was reduced to nothingness . . .

This dream where he did not feel superior to she
And she did not feel intimidated by he
If all races came together as one
Discrimination; none . . .

If the air around us was still pure
Because the trees were not cut down
Or the rivers were still fresh
Due to better ways to rid mineral waste
Or the hole in our ozone layer
Did not become larger each year . . .

Everything could happen right here, right now
This dream of a better place
Something imaginary
Is yet to become so true . . .

Deborah Nanua (18)
Port Moresby International School, Papua New Guinea

A Change For The Good

As I fly around the world, all I can see
Is destruction, sorrow and misery
The cogs are rusting on the Earth
But just think of how much it's really worth

I see litter, rodents and disease all around
A new idea needs to be found
The plants suffer as the burning rain falls
The animals all huddle and hide behind walls

The streets are stacked; there's traffic everywhere
Churning rotten fuel throughout the air
The smoke creeps in like a raging bull
The atmosphere being rotted and the sky is so dull

The air is stuffy as the ozone is defeated
The sun's rays burn as life, retreated
Landfill sites with decay, far and wide
Nothing can stop this relentless tide

But light appears as we realise our mistake
And a new direction our world must take

Smaller engines, a cleaner car
Little things can go very far
Using the oceans' natural waves
To save more energy every day

Using turbines to create a better tomorrow
Then more hope will soon follow
Windmills are not appealing to the eye,
'We should put them offshore,' voices cry

Captured light for every family across the globe
Happiness and joy in every abode
As I come to rest and breathe the fresh air
It's a beautiful world when people care.

Luke Hughes (14)
Pudsey Grangefield School, Pudsey

I Have A Dream

P overty, the problem of the world
O ur lands are choked with this plague
V accines for the weak
E xpedient help for the needy
R wanda is a country in need
T hough not the only one
Y ou can help defeat poverty

N eedy people in need of help
E ntertainment to keep them happy
E xercise to keep people healthy
D estroy this invisible enemy
S top poverty

S top poverty
T ry to help those who need it
O pen your arms to those who need it
P revent this evil beast
P rotect the people in poverty
I want this to stop
N ow, so should you
G o out and help the poor and homeless

H elp to stop this problem
E xercise a care for the world
L et's make the world a better place
P lease help stop poverty

I care
T ime for you to care too

S top
T hwart
O verpower
P overty . . . no longer a problem of the world.

Oliver Bentley (13)
Pudsey Grangefield School, Pudsey

My Perfect Picture

I have painted a perfect picture,
Something I want to achieve,
A world with no disability or discrimination,
Is it too hard to believe?

Remember that pretty lullaby,
About the world your mother used to sing,
But that song is now dying slowly,
Now I've seen the world and what we bring.

Words are as powerful as actions,
Let's change the world we live upon,
So let my words lead to actions,
And let the lullaby live on.

I have a baby nephew,
He is the most loving little boy,
He is so bright and intelligent,
He fills my heart with joy.

He laughs, smiles, cries, just like you,
But Harry has a syndrome - he stands out from the rest,
For his future I worry,
So I strive to complete my quest.

My quest is to make it stop,
To reach into hearts and pull on emotional strings,
To wipe away the cruelty and sadness,
That each and everyone brings.

So now you share my lullaby,
And the picture we can achieve,
A world with no discrimination,
We can do it, if *we* believe!

Charlotte Thornton (14)
Pudsey Grangefield School, Pudsey

Why Does It Matter?

Crying. Screaming. Then silence.
Take a moment and listen to this.
Our eyes are covered by the cloudy mist.
Why be judged?
Why is there pain?

Appearance. Skin colour. Why does it matter?
Different faiths. Why does it matter?
In God's eyes we are all equal
In the quest for peace.

Shoes. Shirts. Hats.
Should this reflect our personality?
My dream . . .
My dream is to see harmony in this world.

Not to be judged.
Not to fear.
Not to feel pain
What do you gain.
By inflicting pain?

Every day. Every night.
Between this, should be peace.
No violence. No anger.
Let there be peace!
Words speak louder than actions.

So, listen to this.
Our eyes are covered by the cloudy mist.
Why be judged?
Pain. Fear. Hatred.
Heart of the world should be free!

Saif Shahidi (14)
Pudsey Grangefield School, Pudsey

Drugs

Oh, my dad smokes cannabis,
I wish he would stop,
Or one day I fear he will drop.

I have a dream that drugs will be banned
And everyone who has used them
Will be locked up and have no toast with syrup.

Now my mum smokes cannabis,
What am I to do?
She started seeing characters
From Teletubbies, just like Noo-noo.

I have a dream that one day all drugs will vanish
And the world will be a safer place and won't be dumb
But I feel that day will never come,
I don't know how long I will last
Until I need a head cast.

My brother is on crack cocaine,
I really hate it,
Cos yesterday he just hit and hit.

My sister's on crack cocaine,
I wish God would punish her,
And change her sex into a sir.

I swear I'm going to kill myself because of their addictions,
I tried to make them talk to Frank,
But they just rang the bank.

Holey moley, they've been arrested,
On charges of drugs,
That will teach them for acting like thugs.

David Burrell (14)
Pudsey Grangefield School, Pudsey

I Have A Wish

I have a wish . . .
That one day animal testing will stop.
People will realise how mean and wrong it is.
Animals die from testing every day!
It's just not right.

I have a wish . . .
That animals will be free from testing.
Animals will be free from cages,
That one day all animals will have loving homes.
Is it right to blind animals?
Is it right to harm animals in any way?
Well, I don't think it is.

I have a wish . . .
That one day nothing, nothing at all will be tested on animals.
That no animal will be harmed.
That there will be a law against it!
Animals have rights, just like us!
They don't deserve to be treated like this.
Not like this.
You wouldn't treat your pet like this.
Would you?

I have a wish . . .
That animals will be loved.
Not to be tested on.
That it will come to a stop, full stop.
That they will find other ways to test products.
That one day animals will live in peace, be free and be loved.

I have a wish.

Lauren Berridge (14)
Pudsey Grangefield School, Pudsey

I Have A Dream

Do you feel safe at home
Sitting there all alone?

They're supposed to love
But instead give you a shove
Act like they don't care
Pulling your hair

Sat alone in your room
In a world of gloom
You wonder why
They don't come when you cry?

Feeling down
The only one in the town
Who isn't cared for
Feel like you want to roar

Full of anger and hate
Just want a mate
Who will understand you
And help you through

When times are rough
You need to be tough
And not be defeated
But instead be treated

Like a normal child
Who always smiled
Do you feel safe at home
Sitting there all alone?

Ruth Cass (13)
Pudsey Grangefield School, Pudsey

A Beautiful Day

The sun's shining today,
What a beautiful day,
Although,
I see a rain cloud,
I see a rain cloud,
What could this mean?
Is God taking away my beautiful day?
Is this because there's still evil in the world,
Hatred, guilt, coldness, stone, fire, war, murder?
These feelings are what we should never have to feel,
What we don't need in our hearts,
So pure,
So warm,
So much love to share,
Why can't we all just care?
Happiness and friendship,
Lead us to a better life,
A life without racism,
A life without hate,
A life without hurt,
A life in a dream,
Full of happiness,
Full of friendship,
Full of love,
Full of warmth,
A dream,
My dream,
Our future.

Ben Prest (14)
Pudsey Grangefield School, Pudsey

I Have A Dream

The freezing cold bites my extremely cold skin
Finding a place for the night is the hardest thing.

Cold on a night and cold on a day
Seems like the frostbite's here to stay.

Last night I got bread!
That's the last time I got fed.

A 'tramp' I am, well that's what they say
You know like they do and then look away.

I've thought about committing suicide
It's just another place where I can hide.

Over there, food on a plate!
I'd better go grab it, I can't be too late.

My box is getting rather soggy now
How did I end up like this, how?

When people look me up and down
I feel like I'm not wanted in this town.

In my sleeping bag I lay
With nowhere I can stay.

All I need is a bit of change
Help me out, I'm not that strange.

Would you like being like me?
This is not a nightmare, this is reality!

Jessica Sanderson (14)
Pudsey Grangefield School, Pudsey

One Day

A perfect world,
A perfect society,
Free from hate,
Free from violence.

Shattered by the state of war,
Devastated by terrorism,
Sacrificed by bullying,
And ended - by us.

We are all the same,
All to blame,
What to gain?
Nothing, but pain.

Severed limbs - war,
Death in masses - terrorism,
Suicidal death - bullying,
Human nature - us.

Naturally evil,
Naturally cruel,
Characteristics of humans
A way of life by mankind.

People don't you see
Or is violence left to be?
Add a full dot stop,
And add a full dot stop right now.

Scott Wilson (14)
Pudsey Grangefield School, Pudsey

Victims Of Bullying

This is for the victims of being alone
And feeling like no one cares
This is for the victims of hurtful words
And sick of all the stares

Talking nastily behind your back
You pretend that you can't hear
But they're threatening to give you a smack
It's more terrifying day by day

Not knowing who to turn to
Maybe teachers, family too?
But, the question is
Will they ever understand what you're going through?

Scared of the clothes you wear
And if you don't fit in
Silly things, even the colour of your hair
This shouldn't be allowed

Laugh along with a bully
You are one too
Stupid little childish games
They don't have a clue how much they're hurting you

This is for the victims of being alone
And feeling like no one cares
This is for the victim of hurtful words
And sick of all the stares.

Lauren Brennan (13)
Pudsey Grangefield School, Pudsey

I Believe

Fighting, violence, anger, hatred, pain, death.
Stop it, I believe.
People crying, people dying.
Stop it, I believe.
People laughing, people smiling.
Start it, I believe.
Happiness around
Not people dead along the ground.
Start it, I believe.
Stop this violence, make it right.
Start it, I believe.
You can still hurt them just by being perceptible.
Stop this pain!
I believe.
Choose the right path.
Or it may lead to death.
Stop it, I believe.
Make the right choice . . .

Because it might not just affect you,
But the people you say it to.

Stop this, I believe.
You can make it right,
Just decide not to fight.
Stop this!
I believe!

Thomas Johnstone (13)
Pudsey Grangefield School, Pudsey

I Have A Dream

One day, hope will be achieved,
Hope will become reality.
Size zero modelling is disgraceful,
All the pain and suffering.
All the pain and fear, for nothing,
Nothing remotely sane.

Size zero modelling is disgraceful,
All the pain and suffering.
Living in fear of a shorter life,
For what?
For the media, the industry?
It's not right!

All the pain and fear,
For nothing;
All of the choices that are made,
We could reverse and be a support,
And help out these nervous girls.
Just by being someone to talk to,
Or a shoulder to cry on,
So stand up to the press,
Stand up to the media,
Stand up to whoever gets in the way,
And be free . . .

Daniel Sheridan (14)
Pudsey Grangefield School, Pudsey

I Have A Dream

I have a belief
A belief that I hope will be achieved
The belief I have is to stop bullying
And for hatred to come to an end.

What if it was you?
Would you like to be bullied?
No, nobody wants to be bullied
Well, before you do it, just think.

I have a belief
A belief that I hope will be achieved
My belief is to stop knife crime
And the violence to come to an end
What if it was you?
Would you like to get stabbed?
No, nobody wants to be stabbed
So before you carry a knife, just think.

Think before you go out
Do you want to be bullied?
Do you want to get stabbed?
If not, just think,
How would you feel if it happened to you?

Matthew Christopher (14)
Pudsey Grangefield School, Pudsey

One Day I Want To . . .

One day I want to . . .
Make a difference.
Help change a life.
Maybe even save a life.

One day I want to . . .
Be heard by the world.
Make an impact on someone.
Whether it be boy or girl.

One day I want to . . .
Bring peace to this world.
To stop all the havoc.
The comments, the violence, it has to go.

One day I want to . . .
Not walk down the street and see.
Someone being bullied.
It's not clever, it's just plain mean.

But, today I want to . . .
See everyone getting along.
Playing together, talking together.
Getting along.

Courtney Jade Teale (14)
Pudsey Grangefield School, Pudsey

I Have A Dream

I wish for, I hope for, I long for a world,
A world without discrimination,
A world where we can live without abuse hurled,
Hurled at us for no reason.

Not only are we being discriminated,
But we are discriminating,
Discriminating over the smallest things,
That make us individuals.

A small minority of people commit suicide,
Due to unfair actions of others,
These people have emotions and feelings,
It's a wasted life, it's a wasted talent.

If you see someone that you don't like, please don't,
Don't abuse them, leave them to themselves,
Just think, it could be you that's being abused,
How would you like it?

Adam Threapleton (14)
Pudsey Grangefield School, Pudsey

I Have A Vision!

I had a vision that one day this world would be benevolent
I had a vision that one day people wouldn't be horrible
I had a vision that one day all the people would be treated fairly
I had a vision today
I had a vision that one day the poor people would become richer
I hope that nice things happen to the world and all the people in the world
I had a vision that one day all of a sudden the world would be better
I had a vision that all drugs should be taken out of this world
Like cocaine, ecstasy, heroin and many more
I had a vision that my family became successful, fortunate, lucky, extraordinary
I had a vision that everyone would learn from their mistakes
I had a vision that there would be no violence
I had a vision that there was nothing but peace in the world
I had a vision!

Jade Niikole Procter
Pudsey Grangefield School, Pudsey

Tolkien, To Tolkien

Tolkien, to Tolkien,
A letter to say thanks,
Thank you for all you've given,
But more to thank you for inspiring me,
My aims and in life what I want to be.

Imagination, your imagination,
What wonders it's created,
Orcs and trolls and the power of the ring,
Your Rohan, Mordor, Black Gates and Mount Doom,
If I had your imagination my life would quickly bloom.

Influence, your influence
You do not even know,
How popular you are,
The books are now films,
And I'm sure you would be proud.

If only, why if only,
I could meet you today,
If I could have a pleasant chat,
And let your influence and imagination,
Cover me and make me smile.

Words, your words,
Like a master blacksmith,
Or a mad magician mixing a potion,
Your words are as magical,
As Middle-earth itself.

Tolkien, to Tolkien,
A letter to say thanks,
Thank you for all you've given,
But more to thank you for inspiring me,
My aims and in life what I want to be,
Thank you.

David Martin (13)
Ratton School, Eastbourne

Nature's Inspiration

Outside in the gentle breeze,
The wind whistles in my ears,
Birds tweet in their nests
And children laugh with big smiles.

I love nature's song,
And the beauty of the world,
Colours bright and meaningful
Inspiring me to laugh.

I'm walking through the leaves,
Scattered on the floor,
Autumn is here,
It's that time of year.

Every leaf unique,
Most of the trees are bare,
But still nature's beautiful,
Looking nice for its visitors.

I come across a path,
And next to it another,
The wind helps me choose,
The path I should take.

At the end of the path,
Past all the fields,
And over the hills,
What a view,
Nature's inspiration.

Chelsea Willgrass (12)
Ratton School, Eastbourne

Disaster Seas

Why do we always go away
On some exotic holiday?
Isn't our footprint big enough?
No wonder our world has got it tough.

So why can't we say what we should say?
Why can't we see what we should see?
Why can't we be like we should be?
We're swimming in the carbon sea!

Why is this fighting going on
Not just day, but all night long?
Doesn't anyone have their rights?
Isn't that enough to spare a life?

So why can't we say what we should say?
Why can't we see what we should see?
Why can't we be like we should be?
Politics is swimming in the crimson sea!

Some people have nowhere to go,
No one to laugh with, no one they know,
They're the ones who have got it tough,
They're the ones who are sleeping rough.

So why can't we say what we should say?
Why can't we see what we should see?
Why can't we be like we should be?
They're swimming in the restless sea!

Aidan Pittman (13)
Ratton School, Eastbourne

Brotherly Inspiration

We always used to scream and fight
I used to shout with all my might
The throat sweets I used to go through!

Me in my room, you in yours
Swearing, hitting, slamming doors
Woah, the tears I used to shed.

I'd try not to look at you for the rest of the day
But you'd be there, all laugh and all play
Yep, you were always that bad.

But, if needed, you'd stick up for me
And in return, my love was free
Deep down there was no real hatred.

Then you decided to join the army and become 'a real man'
Since then you've fought two times in Afghanistan
Yes, it's scary for us, but not for you.

You're hardly ever with us, in our quiet town
So we're always looking forward to when you travel down
You make us so proud.

Now you're a stronger person
And a role model to me
Even after all our rows
You're more than a brother you see.

Rachel Ledner (13)
Ratton School, Eastbourne

Undefined Seeds

A million faces,
A heart in a crowd,
A desperate whisper,
A laugh that rings loud,
A dream that's unbroken,
A blank canvas unveiled,
A glimmer in the darkness,
A lake to be sailed,
A spirit full of joy,
A day filled with hope,
A reflection of beauty,
A sense you can cope,
A wing on a butterfly,
A thorn on a rose,
A smile from a stranger,
A place no one goes,
A bright shining candle,
A last tear unshed,
A new dawn arising,
A life to be led,
A deep inspiration through all that may come,
A feeling of happiness that you're not the only one.

Polly Davis (13)
Ratton School, Eastbourne

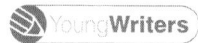

A Dream Like King

Dreams can shape our lives,
Dreams can shape our thoughts.
Dreams can shape beliefs,
Dreams can shape our wants.

Dreams can change our friends,
Dreams can change our dreams.
Dreams can change our countries,
Our minds burst at the seams.

Dreams can change others,
Even those not known.
Dreams will change the world,
Your dreams are not alone.

Think about a person,
A character not a thing.
A person with ambition,
Dream a dream of King.

He dreamt of a nation,
With people free and strong.
A man who would change the world,
And generations to come.

Jacob Bradbrook (14)
Ratton School, Eastbourne

How To Deal With War?

When the world is at war
We must stand together to defeat our enemy,
This enemy will cower in its numbers
But when they are alone
They cower in the evil ends of the Earth.
Together we must rise up and defeat this enemy.
No matter where they come from;
Land, sea or air we shall
Never surrender
Never give up.

We must not let our country become vulnerable to attack.
No matter where they come from;
In our towns,
In our fields,
Or in our streets.

But is this the only way?
Must we fight and must we die?
There is a war we all can fight.
That war is negotiation.

Patrick Gates (12)
Ratton School, Eastbourne

One In A Million

You are the star in my midnight sky
You were the answer when I wondered why
You are the wings that let me fly
You are one in a million.

You are the candle burning bright
You are beside me when I fight
You put my dream close in sight
You are one in a million.

You are the one who guides me on
You give me power - you make me strong
You put things right when I have done wrong
You are one in a million.

For you, I would run one thousand miles
For you, I'd wipe your tears and give you smiles
For you, I'd make every day worthwhile
For you, I'd be one in a million.

Megan Dennis (12)
Ratton School, Eastbourne

World Peace

Imagine it, a world of peace,
No more war, no more fights,
Imagine it, a world of peace,
No arguments between blacks and whites.

Imagine it, a world of peace,
Where religion is not a crime,
Imagine it, a world of peace,
Where everyone is kind.

Imagine it, a world of peace,
Where harmony resides,
Imagine it, a world of peace,
Where people don't choose sides.

Imagine it, a world of peace,
Where mankind stands proud and tall,
Imagine it, a world of peace,
Where love is felt by all.

Lydia Harris (13)
Ratton School, Eastbourne

War

I run through the trees
Through the streets
Through the mud
Through the rain

As a team
As friends
Together till the job is done
Fighting day and night

Will not stop
Till the enemy is dead
Gone, destroyed.

Dominic Baker (14)
Rossall School, Fleetwood

I Have A Dream

In a silent street in Afghanistan,
A boy is dying, not even a man,
He's been shot like a dog,
Lying alone, he is in so much pain,
He can't even moan,
Sent by the Taliban, in a suicide attack,
Ran to the street, a bomb strapped to his back,
But before he could make it, they gunned him down,
Like they would a tin can, this little boy, not even a man.

On a busy London road,
A mother with a child and bags by the load,
Gets on a bus, about to explode,
She does not know, it is normal for her,
Nothing to say, nothing to confer,
All of a sudden, a flash of light,
A noise like thunder, that sounds like God's might,
The bus is nothing but a flaming wreck,
The pillar of smoke is like a huge black neck,
Of the mother and child, nothing remains,
But there are still bombs on buses, planes and trains.

I have a dream that all this will end,
These random acts of terror, that no one can mend,
If those responsible would open their eyes,
Then they might just realise,
The thing they could never, ever tell,
That they're making living on Earth,
Like living in Hell,
Then maybe, just maybe, all this would stop,
Instead of making everyone's safety drop,
They would learn to love, instead of hate,
Then they could greet anyone with the words, 'Hey mate!'

Aidan Parsons (12)
Rossall School, Fleetwood

War

The hopes of many go afar but some of a few wish upon a star
For many a day for death and despair which is unfair
But hope and dream for something else
Which we can only define as health.

Deaths are many
Bombardments a few
How would you feel if it happened to you?
Bang, bang, bang and your life is taken
Or maybe you could be mistaken.

A killer, but for a good cause
They say to their countries
But they should be ashamed
When they take a life
For they are killing their souls.

It is irresponsible, the feeling to kill
Everyone is illegible to take someone's life
Besides on the inside everyone is indistinguishable
On the inside, aren't I right?

Freedom, freedom we shall soon shout out
For I know the executioners at the executions have doubt
Abandon your battle stations
And abort the war.

So let those terrorists do what they will
But we shall arrest them before they can kill
With policemen the best, and MPs too
One day we can all shout, 'Freedom,' too.

Alex Bettison (12)
Rossall School, Fleetwood

I Have A Dream

I had a dream,
It was very bad,
I thought that ET
Was my dad.

He fed me spiders
For my tea,
He made me go
To bed at three.

I told him once,
I told him twice,
But all he did
Was chop up my pet mice.

I said, 'ET,
That's not what you do,
He is my pet!
Boo-hoo, boo-hoo!'

All of a sudden
I heard a *bang!*
I jumped out of bed
And here I am!

I'm in my room,
Safe and sound,
ET is nowhere
To be found!

Ebony Chettoe (12)
Rossall School, Fleetwood

The Rainforest

I see an amazing world full of animals
But I also see it full of horror
They kill these animals
The horror doesn't stop there
They destroy the environment
And this horror is known
As Man.

Man rips down the ancient trees
The monkeys screaming with fear
The birds fly up to the rainy, grey sky
They do anything possible to get away
From the horror.

I see the men with their terrifying chainsaws
With their destructive bulldozers
I also see the tiny animals running scared
Then I see a man tied to a tree
I hear him shouting for
The carnage to stop.

Not all men are bad
Some of them try to save the environment
I some day want to be one
Of these men
I have a dream.

Sam Lowry (12)
Rossall School, Fleetwood

I Have A Dream

I have a dream, anyone can have their dream,
I have my dream, you have your dream.

Dreams are very important for everyone,
If people don't have dreams,
It means they don't have any target to aim for,
So they won't have a future

If you have your dream,
If you want to get to your target,
Then you need to work hard to get the dream,
To get your own target.

Dreams can make you move forward,
Face to front, be immortal,
We're human, we have brains,
We have knowledge, thinking and senses,
Dreams, God gave us the best gift.

Your dream to be a footballer,
Her dream to be a hairdresser,
His dream to be a teacher,
And 'my' dream is to be a scientist.

Everyone has a dream,
Dream, dream, dream,
I believe everyone has a dream.

Edward So (13)
Rossall School, Fleetwood

Sachin Tendulkar

Tendulkar is my hero,
I want to be like him,
Because cricket is my passion,
And so it is for him.

I'm pulling out my bag,
I'm knocking in my bat,
My equipment is almost ready,
And so it is for him.

Spring is in the air,
The daffodils are blooming,
The nights are getting lighter,
And so it is for him.

He strikes the ball so smoothly,
It soars to the boundary,
It seems to come so easily,
I wish that I was him.

Tendulkar is a legend,
He has inspired me,
And when this season is over,
Perhaps he will want to be me!

Harry Andrews (12)
Rossall School, Fleetwood

I Have A Dream

I need to find my grind
To kick my flip
To be as good as everyone should.

I inspire Rodney Mullen to skateboard
To do it just like me
But if I ever did become a pro
I would only want to be me.

Jamie Huckerby (12)
Rossall School, Fleetwood

Nelson Mandela

Free, free Nelson Mandela.

Locked up for several decades,
Just for what he believed in,
A political prisoner
Who was forgotten in time.

Free, free Nelson Mandela.

Made to beg on his hands and knees,
To go to a funeral so he could grieve.

Free, free Nelson Mandela.

He educated many young men in their cells,
After working all day on the blinding rocks.

Free, free Nelson Mandela.

After 27 years he is free,
As the ban is lifted on the ANC

He is free, free Nelson Mandela.

Dylan Jordan (12)
Rossall School, Fleetwood

I Have A Dream

I have a dream to stop all name-calling and unwanted behaviour
That dream would come true if everyone co-operated in the world today
I have a dream that some day
The Earth will be filled up with wonderful environments
Pretty flowers, fresh grass
I have a dream that one day
Global warming will stop
And areas will go back to how they used to be
I have a dream that the credit crunch will finally end
And England will go back to rule the world
I have a dream!

Ella McGuire (12)
Rossall School, Fleetwood

Princess Diana

Princess Di, oh why did you die?
Affectionate, loving and famous too,
Caring for charity with a warm heart,
Oh, I really wish I was like you.

You are as beautiful as a butterfly,
Flying in a summer's breeze.
Fluttering for the press as you were
So popular it seems.
Oh, I really wish I was like you.

You have inspired me with your commitment to charity.
As stylish as you were, you still took care of others.
Donating to others what was yours.
Oh, I really wish I was like you.

You were a devoted mother with your handsome boys.
You were a lonely wife with no Prince Charles.
Hanging on there you were, keeping strong.
Oh, I really wish I was like you.

Lucy Francessca Mary Whalley (12)
Rossall School, Fleetwood

A Dream

A dream is a goal,
A one true desire,
It's a thing that you aim for,
And a thing you aspire,

It's a craving for fame,
To reach for success,
To go to the top,
To go for gold,

A dream is a vision,
A story of life,
The prospect of achievement,
And perseverance,

So if you have a dream,
Which is impossible to do,
Then keep on trying,
And your dreams may come true.

Thomas Gregory (13)
Rossall School, Fleetwood

I Have A Dream

Anyone can change the world,
It doesn't matter if you're rich or poor,
It doesn't matter if you're tall or small,
Anyone can change the world.

Everyone should have a dream,
It doesn't matter if you're young or old,
It doesn't matter if you're boring or funny,
Everyone should have a dream.

No one can stop you from living your dream,
It doesn't matter if you're clever or dumb,
It doesn't matter if you're skinny or fat,
No one can stop you from living your dream.

Never give up on your dream,
It doesn't matter if you're happy or sad,
It doesn't matter if you're nice or bad,
Never give up on your dream.

Helen Tyler (12)
Rossall School, Fleetwood

Angelina Jolie

Most of her life
She has helped folk
From Delhi to Fife
She is special, no joke.

She is Lara Croft
And Mrs Smith
The daughter of Join Voight
Her kindness is not a myth.

With six little ones
To look after
She has got to do tons
And still nominated for a BAFTA.

Oh, what an inspiration
To you and me
How kind and patient
She brings joy and glee.

Sera Burney (11)
Rossall School, Fleetwood

A Young Mermaid

I found a young mermaid on the beach.
Think it must have come from tropical waters
Because its tail and hair
Held shimmery sunshine and aquamarine ocean.

I kept her constantly damp, tried seaweed, sparkly sand
And strings of clams from her neck,
But she became tired, as if to say, I desire
Something you can't provide.

I made a little mound of pearls,
Not unlike those in fairy tales,
But she looked out of place
And was slowly drying out.

If you believed in it I would come
Hurrying to your house to let you share my wonder,
But I wanted instead to see
If you yourself would pass this way.

Holly Lawton (12)
Rossall School, Fleetwood

I Have A Dream

I have a dream
A dream of a boy, he is small and skinny.
This is the only dream he has ever had,
And he wants it so badly.

I have a dream
The boy calling out, 'I would love to be a footballer.'
The greatest footballer in the history of mankind
As he thinks of it in his mind.

I have a dream
I won't give up, it is my ambition!
I'll train hard and play hard
I won't mess this up.

I have a dream
The crowd calling out my name!
The fans going crazy as he has just scored,
As he has just floored in the finishing goal.

Harley Taylor (13)
Rossall School, Fleetwood

What Are Dreams Like?

A dream is like an acorn,
Delicate and small,
But when it grows into a tree,
It's taller than us all.

A dream is like a bubble,
Effortless to pop,
But if it keeps on going up,
It will float up to the top.

A dream is like a candle,
A small light in the dark,
But if it burns for long enough,
It makes a bigger spark.

A dream is just a dream,
A tree is just a tree,
But only we can change the world,
I wonder, is it me?

Amy Sullivan (12)
Rossall School, Fleetwood

I Have A Dream

There is a dream, somewhere out there,
Imagine further, it's just right there.
Hand in hand, keep it safe,
Just keep dreaming, it will never leave,
But wait and pause, not so fast.

I have a dream, it's in my head,
Taken over, kept me going.
My dream is here,
It's becoming quite clear,
Keep listening silently,
Must stay quietly.

My dream is floating all around me,
Still I don't know, what is it all about?
My dream is not perfect, but it suits me,
I'm ready to tell you
But it has just vanished.

Lucie Carter (13)
Rossall School, Fleetwood

A Green World

I have a dream of a blissful green tree
Where children play and run around
I have a dream that all cars will be green
And all the air will be clean.

I have a dream of electric cars and bicycles
People running and jumping in the fresh, clean air
I have a dream of windmills and water wheels powering country-wide
For we have come to the new age of freshness and freedom.

I have a dream of nuclear power past and sun power new
For people to enjoy the new-found fresh air
I have a dream that the Earth will cool down to be like the past
And to carry on to the future.

Harley Howard (11)
Rossall School, Fleetwood

The World

The world is a garden of wonder
The world is like a piece of gold in the galaxy
Its treasures hold secrets
And in secrets hold answers

The answers need questions
And questions need thoughts
And thoughts need knowledge
And knowledge needs commitment

Commitment needs trust
And trust needs friendship
And friendship needs kindness

And kindness is needed for the environment
But where is this kindness?
Forgotten? Locked away? There is only one key
You!

Mark Williams (13)
Rossall School, Fleetwood

I Have A Dream

I have a dream
Of strawberries and cream
With chocolate sprinkled on top.

He has a dream
Of fish in a stream
With lilies growing on top.

She had a dream
To be the best at the beam
But that all came to an end.

I have a dream
To make the world gleam
With happiness round every bend.

Sophie Hockings (13)
Rossall School, Fleetwood

A Perfect Life

I have a dream of a blissful green tree
Where children play and run around
I have a dream that all cars will be green
And all of the air will be clean.

I have a dream that no war will be declared
And hopefully peace will be in the air
I have a dream that everybody loves their enemy
So everybody will be in peace for centuries.

I have a dream that if people die
They can go to Heaven instead of going to Hell
I have a dream that all sins will be forgiven
And everybody will be nice and peaceful.

I have a dream.

Bernard Au (12)
Rossall School, Fleetwood

I Have A Dream

I have a dream to be the world's best athlete
I will win my very first heat
I don't know what I will be
Maybe a runner, a sprinter or even a swimmer

I have a dream to be the world's best rugby player
Maybe a prop or a scrum half or even a winger
I have a dream to be the world's best football player
I will be the world's best keeper.

I have a dream to be the world's best shooter
Maybe a game or a clay pigeon shooter
Incomers, crossers, rabbits and pigeons
I will be the world's best shooter.

Joshua Stone (13)
Rossall School, Fleetwood

Audrey Hepburn

Her flawless femininity continues to inspire.
With the grace of a gazelle and a ballerina's beauty
She carried herself with such poise and style
And her charm was cherished by millions.

Defined by her dignity, taste and flair
Her effortless elegance was simple yet stunning.
Her acting career took to the sky
And soared above the rest like a bird.

Audrey Hepburn was a wonderful woman
Although no longer here.
She lost her battle with abdominal cancer
RIP my inspiration.

Kate Eleanor Chard (11)
Rossall School, Fleetwood

Ryan Giggs

I wish that I could be like you
But I know that won't be true
Your football skills are so unreal
When you score with your back heel

You truly are my inspiration
You sweat blood, tears and perspiration
Man Utd are the best
Far better than the rest.

Twenty-five years you have been a Red
Sometimes scoring with your head
You are someone I want to be
Thank you for inspiring me!

Ryan Allen (12)
Rossall School, Fleetwood

The Balancing Act

If life were a scale . . .
    Time has probably tilted it to a side
Diverse thoughts and minds weighing on another
    As chosen partisans of a class-defining, self-defending team,
Superfluous passion for the 'super' someone
    Venomous acid bites for the 'reserved' foe
Savaging resources for self-sacrificing, evanescing pleasures
    Leaving a little corner of a busy reason for the whole
Gobbling up generations of greenness for waste
    Giving, renewing too few births of trees to save a million lives

    If I could tip the scale . . .
Repaint our windows of the world, of ourselves, of our lives
    Retype the ways we've lived, our life scripts,
Reuse, rethink, remake . . .
    Return to
        The Middle Path

    A central hub of agreements
A heart of all hearts
    A focus where we, everyone, everywhere, *any way, any how*
Are the same
    No more standing at polar extremities of global derogation
Taking all that is needed, but not what is wished for
    Dreaming and fulfilling goals,
While having fun and enjoying the fact of being alive
    Not engrossing in an aspect of life, tucking into a tight, confined extreme
Spread - life - keep doors open, stretching to all opportunities' edges;
    Balanced
Balance your life, balance the world's:
    But never your good deeds,
        Quite empty is the scale of life on that side . . .

Anjida Sripongworakul (16)
Ruamrudee International School, Thailand

Deciphering A Dream

The light shines in
My life surrounds me
It is black and white
I am black and white
I am a vacuum, a bundle of longing
An echo of silence
I squeeze my eyes shut
The seconds tick away
There is no going back
What's left is a void, a blank canvas
No longer a kaleidoscope of wishes
Or a tableau of friendship
What does it mean?
Que Significa?
If my dream had a voice
Would it whisper in my ear?
Would it shout to the world?
Would it fight off my fear?
If my dream had a paintbrush
Would it paint the white away?
Would it mirror the reflection of desire?
Would it show me the way?
All I can know and all I can say
It is a prism reflecting
The truth of my heart, the truth of my soul
The essence of me.

Madhuri Khanna (17)
Ruamrudee International School, Thailand

One In A Million

I have always been a feminist.
I've seen countless women fight for what they desire
Although my peers say, 'What can you do?
You're just one person, insignificant to those that do not know you.'
I wear a proud and confident face.
Although, deep inside, there are two paths I could choose.
I know not where which path leads.

Uncertainty.
It is what most humans fear.
Uncertainty intimidates us.
Nonetheless, when we think about our everyday heroes.
We are often amazed by their contributions to society.
How did they overcome uncertainty?
Uncertainty prevents us from achieving our fullest potential.
Yet, particular individuals have conquered uncertainty and controlled it.
Some have failed, some have succeeded.
Uncertainty has bitten us again.

I have always been a feminist.
I've seen countless women fight for what they desire.
Although my peers say, 'What can you do?
You're just one person, insignificant to those that do not know you.'
I wear a proud and confident face.
I can dream, can't I?
I am insignificant to those that do not know me,
But I can make a difference.

Penphob Andrea Boonyarungsrit (16)
Ruamrudee International School, Thailand

I Have A Dream

I have a dream
To sail the seven seas,
The rocking of the boat
And the feeling of the breeze.
To shout commands in a race,
To find the bearings in a haze,
The whistling of the wind through the rigging
And the crash of the mighty waves.
To watch the whales,
To see the dolphins,
To pray every day
For the pirates to keep away.
The fading orange glow
Of the beautiful sunset,
To watch the graceful seagull
Fly off to the horizon.
Finally into port we sail
With great experiences.
I store my boat away
Ready for another day.

Tom Stubbs (11)
Ruzawi School, Zimbabwe

I Have A Dream

I have a dream
To feed the hungry ones,
To liberate the imprisoned,
To love the unloved ones,
To clothe the unclothed.
I have a dream
And that dream shall go on . . .
To stop wars
All around Djibouti and Somalia.
The cries of lost love
And the cries of pain,
The moaning of innocent children
And the shrieks of evil.
Just imagine, each lurch of the heart
Could save hundreds.
I believe my dream will go on -
After all, Martin Luther King's did.
I have a dream -
A dream to be fulfilled.

Michell Marufu (11)
Ruzawi School, Zimbabwe

I Have A Dream

I have a dream of Zimbabwean peace
And crime to decrease
So it will become a better place.
To have a better country
Where we can live in a good way
And never go astray.
I have a dream to never let go.
All I want is for Zimbabwe to become one.
For people not to fight,
For all to unite
And all as one we shall stand.
Zimbabwe is beautiful,
But no one sees
That there are keys
To open that wooden door.
We now must stand
With each hand in hand
And unite with each other for Zimbabwe.

Kimberly Tomlinson (12)
Ruzawi School, Zimbabwe

I Have A Dream

I have a dream to see a scene
Of pretty flowers and trees evergreen,
To hear the laughter of children,
To see the smile on an old face,

I have a dream to have peace
Amongst this cruel world,
To see a smile and change a life,
To see a rich man share with a poor man.

I have a dream
To hear a bird sing a wonderful melody
For a blind man to see
For a deaf child to hear

These things I dream for
They are the things that make this world today.

Isobelle Pickering (11)
Ruzawi School, Zimbabwe

I Have A Dream

I wish to do the Dakar Rally,
To feel the wind blowing into my helmet,
To see the lone oryx standing in the desert.
Hearing the crowd screaming my name.
Feeling my bike slide in the sand,
Adrenaline pumping.
Riding over sand dunes,
Watching sandstorms sweep away everything.
Seeing riders on the horizon
Making me determined to win.
Vibrating with excitement,
Relief at finishing first,
Joy and triumph,
Shaking fizzy champagne!

Connor Payne (11)
Ruzawi School, Zimbabwe

I Have A Dream

I have a dream to kill poverty
As it has killed many
I have a dream to end Al Qaeda
As it has ended many lives
Leaving black holes in families
I have a dream
Drug and alcohol abuse shall be banished
Just like it has banished us - the young
I have a dream
The world economic crisis shall be overcome
No more bankers' suicides
I have a dream
With your help, I can make it work.

Marcus Philp (11)
Ruzawi School, Zimbabwe

I Have A Dream

I have a dream to sail round Lake Kariba,
To see what is waiting round the corner.
To take on challenges - whatever they may be.
To feel the wind catch my sail
To feel the wind in my hair.
To camp on the water's edge
To go where no one has been before
To take on big waves carried by the wind . . .
To meet new people on the way
To meet the rivers entering this great lake
To cross the Zambezi.
I am ready to go -
I hope my dreams don't fade and die.

Mathew Ferreira (12)
Ruzawi School, Zimbabwe

I Have A Dream

I have a dream to race the Dakar,
Travel on my bike with my support car.
I whiz past nomads, fly over stones
And hope that I don't break my bones.
I would ride all day, not having to stop
Except for a drink when I reach the top
Of that list of people, until the day's end
Then I'll fix my bike before going to bed.
I'll wake in the morning and have some breakfast
Then go on riding until the very last.
After all the days when I come first
Riding in the rally - the worst of the worst!

Riaan du Plessis (12)
Ruzawi School, Zimbabwe

I Have A Dream

Just imagine
We found a cure for cancer
Just imagine
Children in Africa got an education
Just imagine
The end of bullying
Just imagine
The end of racism
Just imagine
Pollution being no more
Just imagine
We could save the world
Just imagine
We could be united in Ireland.

Emmett Curran (13)
St Peter's High School, Londonderry

I Have A Dream

I have a dream
That one day Ireland will become reunited
I have a dream
That cancer will have a cure
I have a dream
That the world will have peace and no wars
I have a dream
That people in Africa will be as wealthy as us
I have a dream
They will have a good education
If this came true
The world would not have to worry about Africans or poor people
If this came true
The world would be a better place
If this came true
They could afford houses, hospitals and caring homes
If this came true
They would have proper transport like cars, aeroplanes and trains
If this came true
Their water would be clean, clear and healthy.

Keaven Brown (12)
St Peter's High School, Londonderry

I Have A Dream

I have a dream that there is a planet not too big, but not too small
And on this planet there is no CO_2 or pollution
Because there is something better . . .
This planet is a green place
Where there is only wind farms for electricity and solar power
For cars, planes and trains, there are no bad or evil people . . .
The only kind of people that live here are kind, loving and caring people
Also on this planet there are these big rainforests
Which spread for miles on end
And also on this planet there are no two people treated differently
I have a dream!

Caolán Cullen (13)
St Peter's High School, Londonderry

Russell Brand

Unique hairstyle
Skinny jeans
Always says funny things.

What you may not know
Is that
He was
Bullied
As a kid.

Overcoming drugs
Must be hard
But he has done it.

Acting is hard
When laughed at
But he can.

Good vocabulary
Helps you be funny
That's why he's got money.

Rhys Nuttall (12)
Studley High School, Studley

I Have A Dream . . .

I have a dream . . .
That violence and horror will end,
That the world can be one,
And religions will be gone.
I have a dream that
Nobody will starve
But no one will be greedy
And everyone will share.
I have a dream that
Knives and guns will only be used for good
And nobody will even think
Of committing suicide and murder.
I have a dream . . .
That wars will be over,
Nobody will fight one another
And jails will be empty.
I have a dream
That families won't fight
And never break apart
And always be as one.
I have a dream . . .
That there is no such thing
As Hell, the Devil or bad luck
And goodwill will spread.
I have a dream . . .
That there really will be
A pot of gold at the end of the rainbow.

Amber Yapp (12)
Studley High School, Studley

It's 30 For A Reason

My name is George,
I am only three.
What happened yesterday
You don't wanna see.

I stopped, looked and listened
But that wasn't enough,
The car came tearing past
And the airbag went *puff!*

The car came my way,
I didn't have time,
The worst thing of all is
I can't think of a rhyme.

Within a snap,
It was all gone,
My life came to an end
And the swing went to and from.

Why oh why, car
Did you end my life?
I didn't even live
To have my own wife.

Now my story is over,
I wish you good day,
Now here comes my friend
Addie, she's coming your way.

My name is Addie
I am only four,
Something hit me
It was the side of a car door.

I was sitting in a field
Nowhere near any car,
I heard a bump and a crash
It came from afar.

It came scurrying in
From just out of sight,
The door flew in my face
I saw a bright light.

Why oh why, car
Could you not let me be?
Yesterday, oh car
You murdered me.

I send you this warning
You drivers out there,
Please read my last note
As if you really care.

Do you want to murder?
It's not very pleasin'
So keep your speed limit -
It's 30 for a reason.

Katie Andrews (11)
Studley High School, Studley

Cancer

This pain in the head was unbearable
And she could no longer bear it.
As she sat in that dreaded hospital
The piercing screams in her head telling
Her it was untrue.

Just two years to live? She was twenty-four
Why should her precious life be taken from her?
One beautiful daughter, who would lose her mummy.
Why oh why had it chosen her?

It was too late for treatment, they caught it too late.
Why had this dreaded demon chosen her?
This life ruiner, this disease, this destructive killer
Now her life had been turned upside down and
Things would never be the same again.

Cara Harrison (15)
Studley High School, Studley

Memories

We're standing there,
Hand in hand,
With the wind singing,
And the trees dancing.

The distance of the noise,
The train gliding down the track,
The noise gets louder, the train gets slower,
And then comes
To a halt.

A journey of half an hour,
A walk of fifteen minutes,
A wait of ten and
A phone call of five.

Stood in the queue,
Watching and waiting,
Talking and laughing,
Now,
Off we go.

The flashing of the cameras,
The sweet smell of chocolate,
The cheerful sights of families,
Spending time together.

The chocolate we ate,
The photos we took,
The memories we made,
What an unforgettable day.

Seven months ago since our trip.
The memories still fresh,
Over 100 miles between us,
And the strong friendship is still there.

I guess you could say,
The memories will never fade,
But as time goes by,
It's going to be really hard,
For me to forget you.

I look at the photos,
I see that I have changed
And it's all because of you.
You're a real inspiration.

Alexandra Eaves (14)
Studley High School, Studley

What Is The Point?

What is the point of ruining my life,
To hurt me and hit me, to punch me and kick me?
You make me feel like I should end it all,
By hurting or hating myself some more!

What is the point of putting me through
This battle of hate, no one to talk to?
I hate the way you punch and kick,
And make me feel pathetic and thick!

What is the point of calling me names
And swearing at me or playing cruel games?
I hate it so much and I want it to stop,
So leave me alone and just get lost!

What is the point of doing it to me?
I am just normal, why can't you see?
If you know that makes me feel bad,
Why can't you stop?
'Cause it's making me sad!

There *is* no point in bullying me!
So give it a rest and let me be,
You're just showing off to your nasty friends,
It makes me insane and drives me round the bend!

You think I am different, I know you do,
But very deep down you know it's just you,
So give me a chance, I know you can,
And let me grow up like any other man!

George Fitzpatrick (11)
Studley High School, Studley

I Have A Dream

I have a dream, a very dear dream
That I will play for a football club
And make my way for England.

I have a dream, a very vivid dream
That the world will be in peace
And that wars have disappeared.

I have a dream, a very thoughtful dream
That people will live together
And will be united as one.

I have a dream, a defining dream
That England, under my captaincy
Will win the World Cup.

I have a dream, an apparent dream
That deaths will be natural
And that guns and knives will be sorted out.

I have a dream, an obvious dream
That people will live freely
Doing good things when they want.

I have a dream, a penultimate dream
That everyone will be equal
No one better and no one worse.

I have a dream, a very real dream
That the future's in our hands
And that only we can change it.

David Sharples (12)
Studley High School, Studley

Life

Life is unique to you
You choose what your dreams are
You choose how you want to come up in life
Everyone has dreams
And no one can change your life but you.

My nightmares in life are -
Will fighting ever stop?
Will people continue to cause global warming?
Will the world ever be problem-free?

Life is full of problems
Decisions you have to make
Life is full of happy moments
But unfortunately evil creeps in too.

You might say, 'I don't know what I want to be when I'm older.'
But everyone has a talent
Something that makes you 'you'
An idea might strike, but your parents might say,
'How can you succeed like that?'
But even a little talent can grow up to be strong.

People commit suicide, but how is this good?
Something was out there that made them lose the will to live
Let's fight good over evil
Life is unique to everyone
So go out and take your rightful place in our world.

Sangamithra Siddhartha (11)
Studley High School, Studley

My Dad, The Retired Policeman

My dad is the best
Brings love and happiness
My dad was a retired policeman
When me and my brother were born
He stopped the job
And went on to the Stratford Council
My dad tries to help anyone from humans to animals
My dad cheers us all up when he comes home
With a big cheesy grin and a big friendly hello.

My dad looks after a lot of people
From his mother to our lovely dog, Chelsea, the giant Great Dane
My dad takes her for walks
And looked after his mother when she was poorly
He even booked a room for her in the hospital
His mother is very healthy and fine now
Because he came and brought her love to cheer her up
He told her to take her medicine
And because he did it so good she got better
That's a job my dad completed
My dad is very friendly to my friends' families
Or anyone from the council
My dad brings the council love and enjoyment to the job
Because he makes it more funny when he is there
With the giggles and the big grins he pulls
That is why my dad is the best.

George Kocon (12)
Studley High School, Studley

Animals

Animals, animals, animals,
Some may be dangerous.
But they are for me,
Tigers rock my socks!
When I grow up,
I wish to work with animals.
Possibly in a zoo,
As head of tigers.
Hopefully!

What I'm trying to say,
Is that I'm inspired to work with animals.
There are a variety of animals that I cherish and love;
Tigers, wolves, horses, birds and gerbils.

If I ever get the chance to work in a zoo,
To be an animal-keeper
I'd treat them like they were the last on Earth!

I have a dream,
That one day I will be the one to discover a new species.
A dream,
That no one else will have!
One dream,
Just one dream,
That inspires me to know everything,
Of everything of animals.

Sarah Louise Elmes (11)
Studley High School, Studley

Why Is There War?

Why is there war?
What is it for?
Soldier running around,
On the rock-hard ground,
And waiting for the man with the gun,
To very slowly twitch his thumb
And send them to Heaven or Hell.

Why is there war?
To you it's probably a bore
There are people who are on the line
Protecting your lives from horror and crime
And death to come
From terrorism
Which would ruin your lives for good.

But war isn't all bad
Because out there in Baghdad
They're solving the world's problems,
With aggressive negotiations
Helping people fix their lives,
Saving them from a gun or a knife,
Giving food and clothes to the good
Saving them from a bad neighbourhood
And they're doing it to save our world.

Ben Crossley (13)
Studley High School, Studley

That's What I Dream

A shared world,
That's what I dream.
Peace and no fighting,
That's what I dream.
A world with no litter,
That's what I dream.
The world to be friends,
That's what I dream.
No religions,
That's what I dream.
To be one,
That's what I dream.
No global warming,
That's what I dream.
Black and white, friends,
That's what I dream.
Water for the world,
That's what I dream.
A loving world,
A clean world,
A friendly world,
That's what I dream.

I dream the world will be one!

Chloe Greaves (12)
Studley High School, Studley

Just Think About It

Just think what it would be like if all the fighting stopped
Just think how good it would be if everyone was looked at equally
Just think to yourself it's not what's on the outside,
It's what's inside that counts
Think how it would be if the world had just one religion
Just imagine what *would it be like?*

Tom Daccus (12)
Studley High School, Studley

I Have A Nightmare . . .

I have a nightmare,
That violence will never end.
I have a nightmare,
That murder will spread across the world,
That guns and knives will always be used.

I have a nightmare,
That animals will die out.
I have a nightmare,
That world peace will never come,
That people will never be equal.

I have a nightmare,
That pollution will destroy the world.
I have a nightmare,
That starving people will carry on dying,
That different religions will cause havoc.

I have a dream,
That wars will end,
That fathers and sons can come home.
I have a dream,
Poor countries can finally enjoy their lives.
I have a dream,
That we will live as one forever.

Beccy Jennings (12)
Studley High School, Studley

My Friends

My inspiration is my friends,
They are always there for me,
Watching over me like God,
Always there for me when I sob,

My inspiration is
    My friends!

Jordon Swingler (12)
Studley High School, Studley

Have A Guess

I don't know who my inspiration is,
It's hard to tell,
But if I want to be a writer,
Here's the poem to tell.
Before he never shows his face to anyone,
Except for his illustrator,
He travelled around a lot,
Hoping his life would get better.
There was woman he once loved
Hoping she would love him back,
But she didn't and broke his heart,
That didn't affect his research.
In his books he says the world is dark,
But if you look hard enough, you can see good,
Even though it's cold and hard.
He just wants you and me to be safe.
The man in this poem is a mystery,
He always is, and alone,
Sometimes that is me,
But we both have a home.
If you still don't know who my inspiration is,
Then I will give you one more hint,
He wrote 'The End'.

Madeleine Hendy (13)
Studley High School, Studley

I Have A Dream

I had a dream that in the future there would be no more war;
The world at peace with each other.
Everyone had an equal share.
No more recession, no more credit crunch,
No more job losses, no more gun crime or knife crime,
Drugs, litter, smoking and death.

Sam Fonyodi (12)
Studley High School, Studley

Say No!

Say *no*, say *no* to cigarettes,
They kill your lungs, and they kill you,
And I'm not kiddin', that's as bad as it gets!
So if someone asks you, 'Ya wanna cigarette?'
Just say *no* and off you go!

Say *no*, say *no* to nasty drugs,
They mess with the mind,
And they mess with you!
So if someone asks you, 'Ya want some drugs?'
Just say *no* and off you go!

Say *no*, say *no* to bullying,
It's not cool, it's cruel,
And it screws up lives,
So if you see it happening, and asked, 'Ya wanna join in?'
Just say *no* and off you go!

Say *no*, say *no* to alcohol,
Under-age drinking is illegal,
It can be addictive like drugs
It can make you sick and that ain't no fun!
So if someone asks you, 'Ya wanna try some?'
Just say *no* and off you go!

Connor Brennan (11)
Studley High School, Studley

My Great Nan Iris

My great nan Iris cooks and loves the outdoors,
My great nan Iris falls asleep and then snores,
She survived both World Wars and has suffered some falls,
She can only see through one of her eyeballs,
My great nan Iris is 95 years old
But I don't care
Because to me she's like gold.

Joshua Barber (11)
Studley High School, Studley

The Best Family

I'm walking down to school with my best friend,
Until I get to the alley end,
I look side to side, no one there,
But I know I'm being watched by a constant stare.

I meet up with my friends, they're very funny,
But then I see the big bully,
He looks at me, I look at him,
I quickly run behind the bin.

Lunchtime, the worst time,
He brings over a great DS but it's actually mine,
Lesson time is almost here,
Now I'm sweating with fear.

I go home that night, scared and alone,
And already my parents are home,
I walk through the door, stiff with fear,
Then my parents ask, 'What's wrong dear?'

They tell me not to get upset,
They tell me not to worry; I have a lot of potential, they say,
They make me realise I can stand up to the bully,
They really are the best family.

Elliott Peat (11)
Studley High School, Studley

I Have A Dream . . .

I have a dream everyone has someone to love
I have a dream there is nothing to kill or die for
I have a dream to share the world, no religion and no Heaven
I have a dream there is no need for greed and everyone lives for today
My last dream is to stop animals and children being tortured
No wars and no threatening
Maybe one last thing,
Everyone is happy for how they are.

Georgina Morgan (12)
Studley High School, Studley

End Of Dreams

I have a dream
Of robots that are run on steam.
I have a dream,
What does it mean?

I have a dream
That no one will be mean.
I have some dreams
Is it what it seems?

We will be as one,
The future has begun.
Nothing is as it seems.
Do you know what it means?

I had a nightmare.
It was quite a fright-mare.
Pollution means
The end of all our dreams.

The moral of this poem is
To recycle all your cannies.
Don't take the Michael
Get off your butt and recycle.

Ryan Traves (12)
Studley High School, Studley

I Have A Dream!

I have a dream that the world is as one.
We all live in peace . . .
No wars, no crimes,
No suffering, no bullying,
No abuse, no racism.
A world where everyone is equal and happy.
Food for everyone, houses for everyone.
I have a dream . . .

Joshua Rogers (12)
Studley High School, Studley

Thank You

You were always there like an unwelcome
Guest
Constantly there saying what you thought was
Best
Closing the door just seems
Impossible
Even walking away is downright
Unthinkable.

Even with you there I'm all
Alone
With no one to talk to and no real
Home
So who do I turn to in my hour of
Need?
With this horrible problem growing like a
Weed.

But then out of nowhere you suddenly
Appeared
Helping me out, getting rid of everything I
Feared.

Natasha Carlin (15)
Studley High School, Studley

Imagine

Imagine having everyone happy, excited, not sad
Imagine having all the children good, not angry or bad
Imagine all the world at peace, no fighting, no killing, no death
Stopping all the gun crime, the knife crime and all the theft.

Imagine respect running through the world like a wild fire
Old and young will sing a song to stamp out all the liars
Imagine having everyone with cheery, happy smiles
Everybody in the world smiles, smiles, smiles.

Joe Moran (11)
Studley High School, Studley

The Author

Pen in hand
She starts to write,
The powerful words spilling
Rapidly onto the page

The chemistry consistently
Spreading out
On the paper
As she inscribes the heart

Beat of excitement and danger in their hearts
She writes,
Scribbling of their love

For each other.
She knows what is to come
But they,
Are unsure

Of their future
With each other
As she decides their destiny
And fate.

Amy Day (15)
Studley High School, Studley

I Have A Dream

I have a dream
That there will be an end to pollution
And not a single flash of war,
Live in peace and unity
And get on with the guy next door.

I have a dream
That the poor in Africa have lots of money,
As natural as the bees are at making honey.

Callum Grummett (11)
Studley High School, Studley

Be Who You Are!

I have a dream that I am who I am.
I don't pretend who I'm not.
I am not afraid to admit it.
I don't care what anyone else thinks.

If you are pretending to be someone you're not,
Stop and think!
Don't pretend, because you're good enough.
You shouldn't pretend,
Take no notice of everyone else.

If you are not pretending, good, carry on like that,
Because you don't want to be no one, you're not.
If they bully you, stand up to them and be strong.

Bullying!
If you are being bullied stand up for yourself.
If they threaten you, tell the teacher,
Don't be afraid, they will sort it out.

The teachers can sort out any bullies,
If it is verbal, physical or cyber.
If they carry on tell the police.

Amy-Jade Fitter (11)
Studley High School, Studley

I Have A Dream

I have a dream that Africa has clean water
To live and be safe and be healthy
There are only people living like we do in proper houses
If we're rich and Africa poor, that's not really fair
Because we can afford food and drinks
But they can't afford anything nice
What if we walk round a track
And for every lap you do Africa gets £2?

Abigail Graham (11)
Studley High School, Studley

My Inspiration

The way he talks,
The way he moves,
He's my inspiration that I chose.

He's not a bully,
Physical, cyber or vocal,
He's my inspiration that I chose.

He doesn't smoke or abuse,
He doesn't take drugs at all,
He's my inspiration that I chose out of them all.

He keeps his money safe and sound,
Which he sensibly uses, when shopping around,
He's my inspiration that I chose.

He helps the environment, animals, plants and the world,
Recycles, reuses and reduces,
He's my inspiration that I chose.

He's a man, successful and truthful,
Talkative and kind,
He's my dad, the inspiration that I chose.

Bethany Middleton (11)
Studley High School, Studley

Poverty

People starving all the time
Try stopping war, hunger and crime
People living on the street
In all sorts of weather; snow and sleet
People surviving with such bad health
While others relax in all their wealth
People made of just skin and bones
While we're only worried about money and loans.

Elliot Evans (15)
Studley High School, Studley

Just Peace

J ust peace for every day
U nder us no Hell
S tarvation ending
T rees won't be cut down

P ollution will be history
E veryone will be fair and share
A nimals won't be hunted
C ountries will come together
E vil will end and goodwill will spread

A lso more recycling
N o global warming
D eath will be natural

N umber of poor will decrease
O ffensive behaviour will stop

W ar will end
A pologies will be accepted
R eligions will be gone

That is my dream!

Kyran Flynn (12)
Studley High School, Studley

I Have A Dream

I have a dream,
A dream to share,
To share what we have
Amongst everyone,
Who is everyone?
Just you?
Just me
Or is it the world?
We must share.
Share what we have amongst the world.
What is it that we have?
Just food?
Just money?
Yes, food.
Yes, money.
Yes, peace, countries, friendship.
We must share,
Share what we have amongst the world.
I have a dream . . .
A dream to be as one.

Caitlin Harvey (11)
Studley High School, Studley

I Have A Dream . . .

Throughout my life with all she has done,
She deserves to live her life with
Good health and to full potential
Not to limitations with her pain.
The times she has spent in hospital,
My mother has failed to give up,
The times she has cried in pain at night.
She has remained positive for me.
Maybe one day the pain will leave her
For doctors will create solutions
To her cysts in her breasts and her hip.
So one day I will be able to
Pay her back for all her support.
So for you, Mum, I just want to say
How much you mean to me and how much
I love you and always will, even though
Sometimes I find it hard to show it clearly.
PS Mum I love you lots and you
Mean everything and the world to me.

Charlotte Elkins (14)
Studley High School, Studley

I Have A Dream

I dream of world peace,
I dream of happiness.
I dream of a pollution-free world,
I dream for friends.
I dream for the world to be one.

I dream of love and care for everyone,
I dream of affection towards other races.
I dream of no war,
I dream of a better place to live.
Don't you?

Jaspreet Kalsi (11)
Studley High School, Studley

Say, 'No!' To Drugs!

We all have a choice about drugs,
We all know it messes with us,
We all know we could have a long jail sentence,
We all know it could lead to crime,
We all have a guide,
But yet we take drugs.

But we can change all of this,
By saying the word, *no*!
One syllable, one word, *no*!
This can change everything from head to toe,
No crime and no guide,
Just your old normal self,

Your life will be really cool,
You might even grab a girl,
We are in this together,
We are in this forever,
Together and forever we can change your lives,
We can change everyone's lives.

Christopher Sutton-Smith (11)
Studley High School, Studley

I Have A Dream

I have a dream for the future
That everyone in the world will have enough food and drink
So no one in the world will die and catch diseases.

I have a dream for the future
That there will be no more war
So no families will have to be distraught all their lives.

I have a dream for the future
That there will be no more drugs
So people won't die, be unhappy
Or have nervous breakdowns in their lives.

Sam Watton (11)
Studley High School, Studley

I Have A Dream

J'ai un rêve.
Tengo un sueno.
R nmero meyty.
Eu tenho um sonho.
Lo ho un sogno.

A dream that will change my life,
And *yours*.
I want the world to be a safer place,
For *you*.
Everyone is equal,
Me and *you*.
Stop the world's crime,
By more than a few.
Many people will not agree,
So it's a short queue.
But the people who do care,
And whose dream is still due,
Act against the others!

Vraj Chauhan (11)
Studley High School, Studley

I Have A Dream

Imagine if there was no cruelty to animals
Imagine if people stopped dropping litter
Imagine if there was no racism
Imagine if there was no crime
Imagine if there were no drugs
Imagine living your life in peace
Imagine if there was no pollution
Imagine if there were no children being hurt
Imagine if there were lots of tigers
Imagine if there was no greed or hunger
This is my dream for a better world.

Jake Preece (12)
Studley High School, Studley

I Have A Dream

Imagine a world without murder
No killing, no violence, no pain
Everyone living as one
Together, forever as one.

I have a nightmare that
Animals will keep being abused
And children will be abused too
So let's all live together, forever as one.

Let's get rid of all our weapons
Our guns, our knives, our daggers
So people can live in peace
Together, forever as one.

My dream is
There will be no more wars
All countries join together
And we will always live
Together, forever as one.

Izzy Runacres (12)
Studley High School, Studley

I Have A Dream

Someone please tell me why everyone's out to kill,
Somcone please tell me why there's no free will,
I have a dream that all countries are at peace,
No fighting or hunger and racism will cease,
I have a dream that prejudice will end
And the poor will then be able to spend.

I have a dream that only we can do,
So let's work together and make things new,
I have a dream that we can stop crime,
And that it's only a matter of time.
I have a dream.

Rebecca Pinfield (12)
Studley High School, Studley

I Have A Dream

I have a dream that the world will be as one,
One happy, clean, healthy and wealthy world.
Imagine peace within us,
In our hearts, in every single one of us,
Everyone equal, all wealthy and healthy.

Imagine a world with no Hell below or no Heaven above.
Imagine your life lasting forever,
A life that will never end.

Imagine a world,
A clean and happy world,
Where everyone lives as one,
One big, happy world.

I have a dream that everyone will be equal,
Nobody more important,
Everyone the same.
It doesn't matter what you look like,
Inside, everyone's the same.

Lauren Shepherd (11)
Studley High School, Studley

I Have A Dream For The World

I have a dream, a dream for the world
A dream that will make the world a better place
And that dream is to make the world fair
Fair in judgement, fair in choice
And for the world to be fair in everything anyone does.

I have a nightmare, a nightmare that I hope will never happen
A nightmare that should stay away in the back of my mind
And that nightmare is war and fighting all over the world
Imagine, a world filled with hatred and hurt
Imagine, everyone fighting against one another
Imagine, the world crumbling at our feet.

Charlotte Roberson (11)
Studley High School, Studley

I Have A Dream

I have a dream to travel around the world,
I have a dream to see amazing places,
I have a dream to meet fantastic people,
I have a dream to help the poor.

Imagine a world where no one is ruler,
Imagine a world where everyone works together,
Imagine a world where there are no countries,
Imagine a world where there's no hate, hunger or prejudice.

I have a nightmare that gun crime won't stop,
I have a nightmare that vandalism will rule,
I have a nightmare that good will come to an end,
I have a nightmare that we will all live in fear.

I've seen a world where everyone is happy,
I've seen a world where no one will kill,
I've seen a world where people help each other,
I've seen a place where people change the world,
So get out there and be that person!

Oliver Harris (11)
Studley High School, Studley

Bullies

What is the point, the point to fight?
They make me feel scared for my life
I'm down and upset
But I will survive
Because I will get them out of my life
I woke up today more afraid
Because of what I did
I'm now ashamed
Please don't hate me for hitting back
I'm so, so sorry
I won't become like that.

Heather Paice (13)
Studley High School, Studley

I Have A Dream

I have a dream to stop all abuse to children
And help them live in a better world.

Imagine all the people living together
And being nice to each other in the world.

Imagine that the world will have peace
And the world will live forever.

I have a dream to stop vandalism.
I have a dream that all the people in the world live as one.

I have a dream that people will not be separated
By the colour of their skin.

I have a dream that there is no Heaven or Hell, just the sky
And we'll be there all together when we die.

I have a dream that the people will not kill or die in the world.
I have a dream that people in the world will not be pressured
To do something bad on Earth.

Bradley Maxwell Manchip (13)
Studley High School, Studley

Poverty

The children sit there,
Starving,
Their distant screams can be heard,
All the way in England
Yet, why does nobody help them?
As disease spreads, they wonder if they're cursed,
They're just unfortunate.
I have a dream that suffering will be over.
I have a dream in which children will be born
With an equal chance in life.
As the children are filled with hope and belief.
Let's hope we can raise money for them, on Comic Relief.

Charlotte Hendy (15)
Studley High School, Studley

A Poem Dedicated To ICT Dave

I draw inspiration from ICT Dave,
As you may know we share the same name.
Whenever a computer is turned off or broken,
When he works his magic, it's like the computer is awoken.

He always seems to be there with his screwdriver,
Opening up the computer and tinkering inside her.
He looks so cool in his leather jacket,
Standing outside the ICT room, eating his packet

Of crisps and a Yorkie,
Carrying around his walkie talkie.
So whenever a computer is turned off or broken,
Call ICT Dave and then the computer will become awoken.

He walks around like member of NYPD,
Wiping out viruses wherever they may be.
He is like a cyber gardener,
Wiping out the weeds that are computer errors.

David Nuttall (15)
Studley High School, Studley

A Best Friend

A best friend is there when you need them the most,
When you stay at their house they should always make toast.
A best friend always listens with their heart,
But never let them hear you fart.
They will always be honest and true
And forever be there for you.
Whether you're feeling bad or even down,
They'll make you smile like a clown.
A best friend is someone who shares a smile,
Someone who brightens up your day
What makes a personal friend
Is saying your love will stay.

Olivia Bampfield (12)
Studley High School, Studley

Grandad

My grandad, at the heart of the family
In my heart, that is where he will always be
A year it has been since he passed away
His faith in God finally set him free

His face portrayed a permanent smile
His jokes which made me laugh were funny
Seven children, thirteen grandchildren; a large family
With him around it made our days forever sunny

At his funeral many people gathered
Tears like crystals swelled in their eyes
Saying goodbye to a special person
Shedding away their bonds and ties

So my grandad wasn't a hero
Just an ordinary person, a saint of his kind
But he was my inspiration, my idol
And his memory will always be in my mind.

Katie Driscoll (14)
Studley High School, Studley

Races, Places, Faces

Racism. The lingering demon, just like the angel of death,
That waits, waits, waits and waits.
In the times of today, it's the law that states,
'People are equal, black, white, Asian, Chinese, all are equal.
Racism waits to create a thrilling sequel,
To what was 'normal' so long ago.
Looking through history there have been many types of separation,
But, none have lingered so long as this.
It may have started as a hollow diss,
But since, it erupted into wars between races.
Races, places, faces, these are the only things that separate.
So until that demon strikes again, all we can do is sit and wait.

Benjamin Buffong (14)
Studley High School, Studley

Write Less, Do More!

I saw a message that said,
'Write less, do more'
I thought about this for a while
'Write less, do more'
Then I thought when I write I do, do more
'Write less, do more'
When you write your message goes across
'Write less, do more'
Prime ministers and Lords
Won't get far without written research
'Write less, do more'
If you stop and listen to their words
'Write less, do more'
Read and let the words absorb into your mind
'Write less, do more'
And after all those words maybe, just maybe . . .
you'll write more and do more!

Stacy Archer (11)
Studley High School, Studley

Bullying

Bullies, bullies, bullies,
Bullies can be found everywhere,
They come in different shapes and sizes,
It hurts when they kick me,
It hurts when they punch me,
It hurts when they call me names,
It hurts deep down inside.
I arrive at school the next day,
They're standing on the drive,
They're watching and waiting,
Ready to start their jibes.

Natasha Vale (12)
Studley High School, Studley

I Have A Dream

Imagine
The world stopping littering
Imagine
No gun crime
Imagine
Sharing the world
Imagine
No religion
Imagine
Peace around the world
Imagine
If there was no Heaven
Imagine
If there was no country
Imagine
All the people sharing the world
Imagine.

Lauren Rooney (13)
Studley High School, Studley

My Grandpa

The person who means the most and inspires me the most,
Is my grandpa.

He acts and does things as if he cares,
Even if he doesn't
Always chooses the right thing,
Through the good and bad
He always comes through stronger.

Through all the things he does in his life,
He inspires me to live mine
The exact same as he has lived his!

Rose Morgan (11)
Studley High School, Studley

You Are Who You Are

'Chocolate bar', 'Sootie', 'Why are you so black?'
Why can't people give me, just a little bit of slack?

Why aren't I trusted? What did I do wrong?
Why do people say I'm as black as King Kong?

I never get picked for the football team,
As the colour of my skin seems to always gleam.

But I take no notice, I'm proud of my life,
Even though people think that I might have a knife.

So if you are out there and you look just like me,
Remember my tip, that this is your destiny!

You *are* a real person; you're just bright and colourful,
You are *not* an alien, in fact, you're very huggable!

So if someone calls you Sootie, or even chocolate bar,
You can just simply tell them, *you are who you are!*

Gemma Ward (12)
Studley High School, Studley

My Grandad

I love you Grandad, you should know that by now
And I'll see you again Grandad,
Someway, somehow.

When you died Grandad,
It was like a thousand knives going into my heart.
And I loved it Grandad when you helped me with my homework
Especially art.

Grandad, I loved it when you used to sit me on your metal knee,
You know, the one that fell off when you fought in the army.

But Grandad, let me ask you a few questions!
When will I see you again, when,
Where and how?

Bethany Harris (12)
Studley High School, Studley

I Have A Dream

For me the world is great
Except when I see bullies behind the school gates
A person getting bullied just for being them
Then I see the shops getting smashed in the same way
I wish the world was better
Never any harm
I wish the world was greater with things for everyone
The world is so greedy right now
I wish it would be better
This will bring more happiness
This world is such a dream, no Hell, no Heaven
Just a beautiful place with colours all around
No place for badness, no it's all gone
I seek a world with happiness and love
No racist things anywhere
So come on and have fun!

Max Vanes
Studley High School, Studley

What If?

What would you dream
If there was no fighting
And everybody got along?
At this rate the pollution will make global warming
And we won't be alive in forty years
So do something, do something
Listen to the Earth
As litter touches the floor
It needs to improve
Help the Earth
By not littering
By not fighting
Just be nice to the Earth.

Dan Dowson (12)
Studley High School, Studley

Grandad

Confidence is the key,
To open the door into his life,
My grandad is the person you see,
He's part of a team, Nanny, his wife,
And, every day I wish you see him in me.

He's always there giving me advice,
Like the role he set for his granddaughters,
'It's not always easy but always be nice,'
Looking after us, keeping all his quarters,
He's decisive, I just wish I didn't have to roll a dice.

His blue eyes, my blue eyes,
His green fingers moving rapidly,
Always there helping me say my goodbyes,
Teaching me to be, who I want to be,
Leaving behind the past of lies.

Charley Casey (15)
Studley High School, Studley

I Have A Dream

I close my eyes and what do I see?
Starving children looking at me
Some people are rich, but most people are poor
I wish I could help them have a bit more.

I close my eyes and what do I see?
A family trying to get free
Children are crying while bombs are dropping
This nightmare is never stopping.

I close my eyes and what do I see?
He is ill and she is weak
They are only three
I think it is normal that my daddy is hitting me.

Holly Turner (12)
Studley High School, Studley

Think Of The Past

Think of something mighty
Think of something strong
Think of something breathing fire
Think of what it looks like.

Think of what it does
Think of what it smells like
Think of what sound it makes
I'm sure it's a terrible roar.

Its scales are as red as rubies
Its gaze a frightening glare
Its breath as hot as burning ashes.

Do you know what it is?
Have you guessed?
It's a dragon from the past.

Ieuan Gibbard (12)
Studley High School, Studley

My Dad!

My dad is great, my dad is fun,
But sometimes he is a pain in the bum.
He likes to play music, he likes to sing,
He likes to moan and likes to whinge.
He has no hair and his belly is round,
But I'm always happy when my dad is around.
My dad inspires me all the time,
I hope he likes the rest of the rhyme.

My dad is awesome, one of a kind
Does stupid things and doesn't even mind
When it comes to music he's a helping hand
He's a massive help to me and my band.
My dad inspired me to write this rhyme
But I must go because it's my bedtime.

Daisy Sabin (11)
Studley High School, Studley

I Have A Dream!

I have a dream that there will be no suffering animals
A dream that nobody will be scared of someone else
A dream that peace will arise from sleeping
A dream that the thoughtless gun crime will *stop*
I have a dream that there will be no religion
And no war.

I have a nightmare, a nightmare that is always in my head
And always shiver when I think about it
A nightmare that everyone will be hungry and poor
Imagine that England will become an underwater country
Think that people could suffer and die
Imagine that all you can hear is screaming and death
Can you imagine this world, this dying world
It's in our hands, *change it!*

Millie Shaw (12)
Studley High School, Studley

The Bully

At nine o'clock I get to school, I stand outside the gates,
Too scared to go onto the playground, where the killer waits,

I look around, I take a chance, I leg it to the door,
I feel a hand behind me, pushing me to the floor,

The killer stands above me, one hundred metres tall,
He's menacing and evil, I'm cowardly and small.

He rips my books into tiny shreds, he devours my morning snack.
Then runs off, leaving me lying there, I know I should fight back,

At nine o'clock I get to school the killer lurks inside,
I stand my ground, I do not scream, I do not run and hide,

I march onto the playground and walk right up to him,
And then I say, right in his face, 'Don't mess with me again!'

Eleanor Oakes (11)
Studley High School, Studley

Just Smile!

Today the world has overturned
A smile into a frown.
Today the world has really burned
The love that was around.
Today the world has made
A flower, a dull bit of hay.
Today the world has made to fade
A yellow into grey.
Tomorrow the world will shape and mould
A work of art to clay.
Tomorrow the world will cut and fold
The papers on how to play.
No more the world should beguile
I wish everyone would just . . . smile!

Lauren Rogers (14)
Studley High School, Studley

I Have A Dream That . . .

I have a dream that . . .
The guns and the violence will stop
And everyone will get on with one another
There'll be no murdering and no theft or selfishness
No war with other countries
Imagine a prison only big enough for two people
And there is only one prison in the country
What if there was no Heaven for the good people to go to
And there was no killing or anything to die for
Everyone should go and do something good for someone else
And take a chance to make things better
If you make a mistake
The world wouldn't last without firefighters
And the police and doctors.

Ryan Bourne (12)
Studley High School, Studley

I Have A Dream!

I have a dream that there's a lot less knife crime!
No more stabbings . . .
So that we don't hang off a very thin lifeline.
I have a dream that no one gets let out of prison
Because of good behaviour!
No more escapes
Because we haven't got a brilliant saviour!
I have a dream that people live in peace,
No more nightmares!
The world should be as one instead of having a big crease.
I have a dream that there's no need for greed or hunger,
No more starvation . . .
So young people live their lives longer!
That's what I dream!

Emily Wood (12)
Studley High School, Studley

Fourteen Years

Chapter fourteen, the sky burns white,
Bitterness within, piercing my tongue,
Manipulating me, controlling me.
My obsession, my addiction, my life,
Days fade like colours,
My mind becomes a reality.
I choose to fall, here goes nothing,
The world erased by a curtain of colour,
Crystals crash, crushing.
The sun rises, the blinds unfold,
I know, I cannot rewrite my beginning,
But I can decide . . .
My end.
This is my life, this is my mistake.

Joseph Ashraf-Powell (14)
Studley High School, Studley

Freedom

Freedom for immigrants
Freedom for the poor
Freedom for black people
Freedom evermore.

Freedom for the religious
Freedom for the humble
Freedom for the homeless
Freedom for all people.

Freedom for all people
On every continent and every country
Freedom will change the world
We shall all live together in harmony.

Sam Rogers (12)
Studley High School, Studley

My Best Mate

Every day we would play,
With jumpers as the goal.
Always bushes in the way,
And the weather always cold.

Running left, running right,
Dribbling down the wing.
Shooting at every sight,
Waiting for the trees to sing!

To find me at my very best,
Football is the gate,
With every touch there's a test,
Me and my best mate.

Lee Palmer (15)
Studley High School, Studley

My Grandad

My grandad's funny and active,
He likes to play with words.
He also likes to dance around,
And play a lot of games.

My grandad's really happy,
He plays around a lot.
I really, really like him,
He brightens up your day.

My grandad's really kind,
He's also really healthy.
He has a clever mind,
So that is why I love him.

Daniel Jackson (11)
Studley High School, Studley

Say No

Say no, why should you put up with it?
You've done nothing wrong.
Tell someone, anyone, you know it's not right.
Stop it now before it takes flight.

Whether it's physical, verbal or cyber,
It's still so cruel.
So do something, do it now!

Why should they make you depressed.
Unlike the rest?
They have no reasons, they have no joy.
So do something, do it now!
Say no to bullying.

Josh Lawrence (12)
Studley High School, Studley

School Dream

My kids, your kids, all the kids around
Smiling, happy faces, happy, laughing sounds
Some think it's boring, some think it's cool
But all the famous people, they all went to school.

You may think it's dull or just a waste of time
But it keeps the kids out of the guns, the gangs and crime
Imagine working where you loved, living a happy life
Having lots of life skills, yet no need to have a knife.

I have a dream
My dream is knowledge, everyone is learning and proud to
With children sharing their experiences
With each other, with me and with you.

Charlee Churchill (12)
Studley High School, Studley

My Poem

My dream is for the people to get along.
No war, no bombs! I wish people could all be friends
And have a happy life.
Why are there wars?
How did the world come to this mess?
What can we do to improve the world?
Where does all the bad language come from?
When is the world going to end?
Stop, think.
We could change the world from ending.

Sophia Cleverley (13)
Studley High School, Studley

I Have A Dream . . .

I have a dream . . .
To be a nurse one day
My uncle is a nurse
He inspires me
To help others.
But the one who inspires me most
Is my nan.
She's clever
She's great
And she knits as well.

Hannah Dixon (12)
Studley High School, Studley

They Stand

She stands there alone,
Solitary and invisible,
She holds a shield; a world of her own.

He stands there alone,
Solitary and invisible,
He holds a shield; a world of his own.

They hold a world of their own
A shield to share,
Invisible together.

Sophia Morgan (15)
Studley High School, Studley

I Have A Dream . . .

I have a dream that only I have seen
To stop pollution and find a solution
To all the problems in the world

I have a dream that only I have seen
That there is no racism, no greed
And no people living on the street

I have a dream that only I have seen
That there is no crime, no murder, no theft
And the world is as one.

Sam Ali (12)
Studley High School, Studley

I Wish . . .

I wish . . .
That there were no wars,
That everyone obeyed the laws,
That no one sprayed the walls bright colours.
That no one ever murdered others.

I wish . . .
That trees would all grow nice and high,
That no one ever let them die,
That everyone was equal, no one was the best,
Who cares who is what colour?
No matter east or west.

I wish . . .
That no one died from lack of money,
That everyone was clever and funny,
No more litter on the ground,
No global warming for miles around.

If we work together, yes, I'm talking to you,
We can make a difference, make my dream come true!

Emily Green (12)
The Ladies' College, Guernsey

I Have A Dream

It is hard to imagine,
In our perfect lives,
Staring death right in the face,
At its dark, enthralling glare,
As we slowly
Slip away.

In our nightmares maybe,
The thought could stir,
Yet we'll stare absent-mindedly at the fact
That for some this is reality,
This is life,
This is death.

At this very moment,
Deep in the heart of Africa,
Someone's eyelids are slowly closing,
Their lungs gasping in their final breath,
Before they sink deep into a dark abyss . . .

Can you imagine your life flashing before your eyes?
Thinking of all your aspirations,
Everything you wanted,
Left unfulfilled,
With nothing you could do about it?

Well I have a dream,
A dream of hope,
A dream of happiness,
The dream that will change the world,
That those people shouldn't have to die.

I see their eyes opening,
Not closing,
Not slipping away from their lives,
Opening to a new world,
Where they will be as rich, healthy, and happy as us.

If we take a leap of faith,
My dream may come true,
Their dream may come true.
So let's reach out and help them

Live their lives.

It is hard to imagine,
In our perfect lives,
Staring death right in the face,
At its dark, enthralling glare,
So let's make sure,
This will not be them.

Sarah Brereton (12)
The Ladies' College, Guernsey

I Have A Dream Mr Fritzl

Why did you do it Mr Fritzl?
You left her there on her own.
With seven children to look after,
And a cellar for their home.

Locked away for twenty-four years,
No sight of the clouds and the sun.
Miserable with no enjoyment,
She forgot the meaning of fun.

Men like you should be locked away,
Punished for everything you've done.
Men like you are despised everywhere,
That's why you're in prison, with how many friends? None.

I have a dream Mr Fritzl,
That men like you are gone.
I have a dream Mr Fritzl,
That you'll have time to regret what you've done.

The world should be peaceful and calm,
The world should have people who mean no harm.
The world can't be perfect, even I know that,
But *you* can help and that's a fact.

The world could *not,* and should
Be free of hate.

Lauren Nicolle (12)
The Ladies' College, Guernsey

If I Created Earth

If I created Earth and made up everything
Here are a few of my rules that would change
The whole thing.

There would be no pollution,
The world would be clean,
We would recycle all our things including
Tin cans, bottles and even rubber rings.

Wars would be banned,
Fights not allowed,
No one would be cruel,
And animals would be safe and sound.

Everyone would have money,
Nobody would live on the streets,
Lots of food for all,
So we would all be happy indeed.

The credit crunch wouldn't be bad nor sad,
It would be very good.
We would gain not lose,
So we could all pay our bills.

Nobody would be hurt,
No one would get killed, just friendly smiles and kisses
To be shared around my world.

All these things and all these rules I have just made up,
But because I have a dream and believe, I'm sure,
With your help we can change our world.

Sophie Hunt (11)
The Ladies' College, Guernsey

Untitled

I have a dream
That child abuse stops,
And it stops now!
No more unloved
Uncared for children
No more screams and violence
No more tears and blood.

I have a dream
That the end of child abuse starts
And it starts now!
More loved
Cared for children
More happiness and joy
More cuddles and kisses

I have a dream
And this dream
Will help change the world
And teach us to live in harmony
To help each other
Not harm each other
And help change the world together

I have a dream
That people will stop,
Stop ruining the future generation
And join hands with them instead.

Bethany Schmiedhuber (12)
The Ladies' College, Guernsey

Poverty

The world is a face,
Full of emotions that no one can race.
Happiness, sadness, it changes through time,
In one place there's adventure, another there's crime.

No one can stop this, it's how the world goes,
People have friends and people have foes.
But there is something that shouldn't be,
Because anyone can help stop poverty.

People with hunger that need something to eat,
People who are tired and need somewhere to sleep.
People that can't afford a good education,
And people who can't afford medication.

Why shouldn't these people have a good life
Just like us without any strife?
Why shouldn't these people survive till the end,
Make it around the very last bend?

The world is a face,
Full of emotions that no one can race.
Happiness, sadness, it changes through time,
In one place there's adventure, another there's crime.

But while this is happening,
Somewhere out there,
People who have poverty,
Need someone to care.

Alice Sarre (12)
The Ladies' College, Guernsey

I Have A Dream

Every day I look around and see
Cars and fumes and a colourless scene before me.
Everything is dark and grey
Full of litter and cloudy days.
The beaches filled up with pollution
There seems no solution.

Forests are destroyed by acid rain
People are starving and dying in pain.
All I see is anger and suffering
It is so disappointing
There is no hint of happiness in every single mile.
When I pass people they don't smile.

I dream of a world that is clear and bright,
With no darkness but burning light.
Palm trees and glorious mountains with flowers
Lots of sunshine with few showers.
No starving or anger or dying in pain,
But dancing and happiness and gain.

I dream of beaches with crystal-clear waters,
And everyone helping keep them clean.
Everyone with a happy smile.
And colour lighting every mile.
No cars or fumes or colourless skies,
But trees and bees and butterflies.

Elise Bisson (12)
The Ladies' College, Guernsey

Goodbye And Good Luck

Off to a war zone
Sadly what might be left
Of them is one bone
Goodbye and good luck.

They are fighting a battle
That could go on for years
But this job they must tackle
Goodbye and good luck.

They want you to be home
All your family are sad
But you can't moan
Goodbye and good luck.

This is something you might not win
There could be more of them
And committing murder is a massive sin
Goodbye and good luck.

So don't go
Goodbye and good luck
But sadly though
You don't have a choice

Farewell
Goodbye and
Good luck.

Natàlia Tanser (12)
The Ladies' College, Guernsey

I Have A Dream

I have a dream,
That the world is a better place.
I have a dream,
That poverty is no longer.
I have a dream,
That global warming will stop.
And I have a dream,
To change all this.

I have a dream,
That people can get better education.
I have a dream that wars are no longer.
I have a dream,
That bullying will stop.
And I have a dream,
To change all this.

I have a dream,
That we can all come together.
I have a dream
That pollution is no longer.
I have a dream
That the credit crunch will stop.
And I have a dream,
To change all this.

Lydia Downing (12)
The Ladies' College, Guernsey

I Had A Nightmare

I had a nightmare.
I heard wildlife crying out for help,
The squirrels and birds looking for their lost homes
But all they could find were the stumps of dead trees.
Those few trees that did survive were dying,
Coughing in the thick fumes from our cars
And trying to pull the plastic bags off their fingers.

I had a nightmare.
Of fish being strangled by our rubbish
That we tossed carelessly in the sea
And even unfortunate little plants
Are getting harmed by air pollution.
We are getting harmed as well as all of this and more;
Tiny children to pensioners and even unborn babies.

I had a nightmare.
Where I saw the world in need -
In need of our help, our love,
To make it better again.
But when I woke up
One word made me smile
To get us to the future -
Hope.

Anastasia Cross (11)
The Ladies' College, Guernsey

I Have A Dream

I have a dream,
Of a world that is clean,
Of no pollution in the air,
Where everyone has care.

I have a wish,
Of a clean sea and fish,
Of animals alive,
Where all can survive.

I have a hope,
That people can cope,
With money so low,
Through the crisis that won't go.

I am worrying,
About people who are hurrying,
Away from the gangs
Who are setting off bangs.

The world will one day,
Turn around and say,
'Work as a team,
You had the dream.'

Phoebe Morgan (12)
The Ladies' College, Guernsey

I Had A Dream, Or Was It A Nightmare?

I had a dream, or was it a nightmare?
I dreamt of the world as a dump,
Litter everywhere, no one to trust
People were screaming,
People were running,
Running away from the fear that they kept locked inside them,
People were hiding,
Hiding from what they felt wasn't imaginable
This was it
A world of pollution
A world of things unimaginable, a disgrace.

People were starving,
Nowhere to sleep
Just a corner of the street.
Maybe an awning if you were lucky,
But if you were not, it was disgustingly mucky,
Do you want this to happen to you?
If not, *we* have some work to do.

Fleur Nicolle (12)
The Ladies' College, Guernsey

I Had A Dream

I think the world should be fair.

H ave money, a house and life.
A nother day shall be beautiful.
D ays where no one is hurt.

A nother day everyone will be together.

D reams like these will come true.
R eally, truly they will.
E arth will be made of love again,
A nd everyone will be happy.
M aybe. Let's hope it will.

Eleanor Atkinson (12)
The Ladies' College, Guernsey

I Had A Dream

I had a dream . . .

To stop war in this world,
To make peace between countries.

I had a dream . . .

To stop people cutting down trees,
To leave them standing.

I had a dream . . .

To stop wasting oil and coal,
To use the wind and waves.

I had a dream . . .

To let animals run free,
To roam the world.

I had a dream
To make the world
A better place.

Elise Dorey (11)
The Ladies' College, Guernsey

If The Playground

If the playground is a cake
Then always under layers of automatic beams
Is a child being bullied
And the bully gleams.

If the playground is a face
Then the bully is the mouth and ears,
As it spreads rumours around
Of the child's worries and fears.

If the playground is a book
Then the bully is the unknown text
Which the child is trying to read,
Trying to sort out their lives, but not knowing what to do next.

If the playground really is all of these objects
Then I have a dream today,
That the playground will become a playground,
Not for bullies to bully, but a place for kids to play.

Anna Ogier (12)
The Ladies' College, Guernsey

I Want A World

I want a world,
Without poverty,
No deaths,
Not a tragedy.

I need a world,
With countries full,
People alive,
Alive and full.

I have a world,
With no caring,
For those who dare,
To make a living.

I want a world,
Without poverty,
No deaths,
Not a tragedy.

Alice Hudson (12)
The Ladies' College, Guernsey

I Have A Dream

I wish that everyone could be neat and tidy,
Putting rubbish in the bin.
Believing that we could do this together
Everyone from grans to kids.

I wish that everyone was equal,
No one would be better.
We would spend our time helping people,
Like we should anyway.

I wish everyone cared,
Caring for each other.
Like a big family,
Everyone together.

If I had a dream,
I would dream all these things,
I would love to think it was real,
If I had a dream.

Alisha Crocker (11)
The Ladies' College, Guernsey

Change

If you could change one thing, what would it be?
The simple environment, or you and me?
The credit crunch or my little bunch of problems tucked together?

Martin Luther King changed the 'bling' of people stuck together.
He changed the world of black and white and turned it into light.

If you could break one rule, what would it be?
The money, the government, or you and me?

Every choice changes worlds.
Changes people by the number.
Every speech, every book.
So do something different.
Do something strange.

Change all the people.
Change all their brains.

Florence Richards (11)
The Ladies' College, Guernsey

Equality

I have a dream, and I wish,
That poverty did not exist.

It may come true, if people care,
But *no one* is prepared to share.

All their selfishness and greed,
But some people are in real need.

I am sure if people tried
Every four seconds, someone won't have died.

There doesn't have to be war for peace,
Yet I still don't see it cease.

If racism did not exist,
I would not be writing this.

Eva James (12)
The Ladies' College, Guernsey

I Wish The World Was Like This

I have a dream,
That all the streams,
Can be all fresh,
Not touched by flesh.

I have a dream,
That all the wars,
Shall always end,
So no poverty soars.

I have a dream,
That cars are banned,
That harmful gases,
Will be used no more.

I have a dream,
Religions mix,
All people are kind,
And friends are made.

I have a dream,
All animals are free,
No endangered cries,
Are harked in skies.

I have a dream,
No one seems poor,
Everyone has water to drink,
All people have food.

I have a dream,
All mammals have homes,
All bricks are used,
All houses - homes.

I have a dream,
All smoking dies,
Smoke leaves the skies,
The cigarettes go.

I have a dream,
All bullying ends,
The children grow,
All people laugh

I have a dream,
Global warming goes,
The skies turn blue,
All birds are out.

I have a dream,
The seas are clean,
Pollution, oiling,
All disappears.

I have a dream,
All birds are free,
They soar the skies,
Outspread their wings.

I have a dream,
All poverty goes,
Starvation leaves,
Hunger starves.

I have a dream,
All nations rise,
The parachutes,
All fill the skies.

I have a dream,
All Christmases,
All sleigh bells ring,
All choirs sing.

I have a dream,
All hands rise up,
All friends belong,
To everyone.

I have a dream,
All disabilities,
Are cared for,
Never left outdoors.

I have a dream,
Petrol is eco-friendly,
No gas let off
The world is saved.

I have a dream,
All wild animals,
Will have homes to lie,
To rest the night.

I have a dream,
On all aeroplanes,
Satellite navigations,
Are done by him.

I have a dream,
That God'll appear,
He'll bring good news,
To help us out.

Bethany Heddle (11)
Tomlinscote School & Sixth Form College, Frimley

I Have A Dream

Like any other usual day I go to school,
It never really seems that cool,
Amongst everyone we don't take it seriously,
The teachers think mysteriously.

Other places in the world,
Children think we are lucky,
If they stood in my steps their life would be uncurled,
But at the moment they feel yucky and mucky.

I have a dream,
(Probably have to work as a team),
But I want all children to be happy,
Not sad.

Charlotte Mandell (12)
Tomlinscote School & Sixth Form College, Frimley

Trip To Dreamland

I have many dreams and aspirations
So many things I want to achieve
To carry out many explorations
And never feel the need to grieve

I want to have fortune and fame
Do something no one has ever done
So everyone will know my name
I want my moment in the shimmering sun

I want to be treated like a queen
Pessimistic and sorrowful I shall not be
This will raise my self-esteem
Everyone will look up to me

I want to be able to change the world for the better
To get rid of hatred and war
My dreams will never fetter
I'll stop prejudice, poverty and more

I'll always be able to speak my mind
I'll always try to be myself
But courtesy and cordiality I shan't bind
I shan't put morality on the shelf

My biggest goal, wish and dream
The one I shall try to achieve
Is to do my best and take the cream
In myself I'll always believe.

Shira Sokolov (12)
Tomlinscote School & Sixth Form College, Frimley

In This New World

I want to change the world,
Make it a better place.
I won't do it on my own,
I'll have help from my friends.
It won't happen overnight,
But it will happen soon.
I shan't have violence,
In my new world.
When I change the world,
Everyone will be happy.
Animals and humans
Will live peacefully together.
People will not be judged
By the colour of their skin.
When the world is changed,
There will be a worldwide cease-fire all year long.
People in Africa will have food and water
When we start this new world.
Politics won't matter,
In this new world.
Everybody will be equal,
Nobody will be different.
In this new world, nobody will be better than anyone else.
In this new world.

Abigail Russell-Samways
Tomlinscote School & Sixth Form College, Frimley

I Have A Dream

I have a dream
Where sunlight drifts down in beams,

All war shall cease
And there will be forever peace,

Chocolate waterfalls will gush
From the jungle - quite lush,

If only you could see
T'would be like Willy Wonka's factory,

The joyful birds would sing
Bringing joy to everything,

With chirping here and twittering there
Birdsong would fill the very air,

My dream shall also contain
The rightness of rain,
Then there will be me
Sitting in a large oak tree
Watching the scenery
Peacefully,

I have a dream
And you just read it.

Brogan McCawley (12)
Tomlinscote School & Sixth Form College, Frimley

When You See A Picture

When you see a picture and you look at it closely.

When you see a picture and you look at it closely
You can change the world.

When you see a picture and you look at it closely
You can smile.

When you see a picture and you look at it closely
You can jump, jump right into that picture and you find
It's not a picture, it's a piece of art.

When you see the art and you look at it closely.

When you see the art and you look at it closely
You can change the world.

When you see the art and you look at it closely you can smile.

When you see the art you can jump right into the art
And find it's not a picture, it's not a piece of art,
It's magic, magic
Fingers to hold the paintbrush to paint the piece of art.

Sasha Mitchell (11)
Tomlinscote School & Sixth Form College, Frimley

Look At The World

When you step outside what do you see?
Just concrete?
On a stormy day what do you see?
Closed curtains? A television screen?
On a long journey what do you see?
The car in front? Your steering wheel?
Or do you look at the world as a beautiful place,
And see birds, trees and people?
A wonderful storm of thunder and lightning?
The blue blue sky and the fields you pass by?
Do you look at the world?
Or ignore it?
Look at the world and see the natural beauty and wonder
Around you
Look at the world as the world,
Not at an everyday sight.
Look at the world as the world deserves to be looked at,
Look at the world.

Nicola Evans (12)
Tomlinscote School & Sixth Form College, Frimley

I Have A Dream

I have a dream
That one word can change the world
I have a dream
That there is one word in the crowd
I have a dream
That in spring all the leaves on the trees will fall
I have a dream
That all the soldiers at war will come home
I have a dream
That one day all the racism will stop
I have a dream
That everything bad will go away
I have a dream
That one day all cruelty to animals will stop
I have a dream
That all people will be friends no matter what the colour of their skin

I have a dream.

Emma Walmsley (11)
Tomlinscote School & Sixth Form College, Frimley

I Have A Dream

All I want is my dreams to come true,
No more wars around my home,
No more living all alone,
No more racism to do with me!

All I want is security,
No more searching around for food,
No more streets to take my rest,
No more looking after me!

All I want is to be safe and well,
No more worrying about the sun,
No more relying on my crops,
No more starving family!

All I want is the world to be free,
No more starving or poverty,
No more death or deadly disease,
Everyone to share a life like me!

Louise Brisk (12)
Tomlinscote School & Sixth Form College, Frimley

I Have A Dream To Change The World

I have a dream to change the world,
I have a dream to make a difference,
I have a dream to help poor people,
I have a dream.

I have a dream to work around the world,
I have a dream to make people happy,
I have a dream to protect my family,
I have a dream.

I have a dream to stop pollution,
I have a dream to stop violence,
I have a dream to stop crime,
I have a dream.

I have a dream to stop racism,
I have a dream to stop the bombs,
I have a dream to stop the guns,
I have a dream.

Hanifah Hashim (11)
Tomlinscote School & Sixth Form College, Frimley

My Dream Of A Perfect World

I dream of trees made of stacks of pies
A world full of laughter
Where there are no lies

Sunsets blaze like fire
Ice has a diamond's sheen
Bad things were never invented
There's no such thing as mean

There's nothing that is dangerous
There is much respect
Everything is lovely
I don't know what to expect

My dream world is so perfect
Flowers are made of gold
I do wish I could live there
No one would ever grow old.

Ryan Truesdale (11)
Tomlinscote School & Sixth Form College, Frimley

Save Our World

Change the world
Go green
Because every day
I wonder
When I'm sitting in my room
How are people coping
Young carers
And the rest?
I wonder how they're coping
With war and all the rest.
I'm not sure how they're coping,
Let's hope
Money raised is well spent!

Yasmine Turner (12)
Uplands Middle School, Sudbury

Our World

I have a dream,
For our world to live in peace.
A world without wars and suffering,
A world where you can feel safe,
A world where you know nobody is going to hurt you.
That's the type of world where I want to live.
Not the type of world where you get hurt for being who you are.
Kindness makes the world go round.

Hannah Woodward (11)
Whitburn CE School, Sunderland

A Vision In The Sky

My vision may probably fail,
As it starves in a drought so dry,
But somehow though it will prevail,
My friends, it's flying sky high.

Of what I see, I fear I must not
Foresee the path ahead,
Most will stay to face a shot,
I'll take care of steps I tread.

Then in my mind I see some wings
Her metal that shines in the sun,
She's followed by a fleet of things
With rotors, engines and guns.

The British stand from their praying knees,
As miracles have been shown,
A C130 Hercules,
Our sons are coming home.

We watch forgotten faces
As eyes fill up with tears,
An escape from violent places,
The peace is finally here.

Robin Hawes (12)
Woodbridge School, Woodbridge

I Have A Dream

Have you ever thought, when you stand there deciding,
Whether you should get it in black or blue?
Those other children out there are mercilessly hiding,
From death.
When you push aside your broccoli, with a desperate moan,
Other children out there are sparing an old bone.

This has to change.

Have you ever thought about acting what you do?
You say you will but I know it's not true.
All those desperate people you see in all those photos,
Are lying on some dust when you're lying on the sofa.
Just think about those lives that you could change.

This has to change.

Have you ever seen a photo of a refugee,
With white people?
You can make a difference
You can rise up the steeple.
Think of the hero you could become,
Think of the world when your work is done.

This has to change.

You are the people of tomorrow,
Start a charity, start a school, build a well,
Anything.
Nelson Mandela expects no sorrow.
You will hear the ringing of the emergency bell.
Don't leave it till later.

This has to change.

Do you know how many people die each day?
Every 17 seconds a child dies in play.

This has to change!

Ella Kiley (11)
Woodbridge School, Woodbridge

I Dream Of A World Where Money, Is Nothing

I dream of a world of happiness,
Where everyone will give and share.
I dream of a world where there is no evil,
Where everyone does care.
But most importantly, I dream of a world,
Where money, is nothing.

I dream of a world where people will do their jobs,
But not for money, for the good of other people.
Where teachers will teach for the happiness of children,
Builders refuse to be paid to mend the steeple.
But most importantly, I dream of a world,
Where money is nothing.

There be no robbers, there be no thieves,
As you cannot steal from people so willing to give.
You give and share with someone and they will do the same,
And a happy life we all will live.
But most importantly, I dream of a world,
Where money, is nothing.

I dream of a world where you can have what you want,
And you don't need to buy it because it is given.
No one pays for food or other things,
Because even if you do wrong you will be forgiven.
But most importantly, I dream of a world,
Where money, is nothing.

I dream of a world where there are no arguments or fights,
Where no one is told what to do.
No one is punished because no one does bad,
Where everyone does what they should, even you.
But most importantly, I dream of a world,
Where money, is nothing.

Saffron Eziashi-Dobie (11)
Woodbridge School, Woodbridge

My Vision

My vision,
Imagine a world with no wars,
People living in peace,
No bloodshed, that is my vision.
Imagine,
Imagine.

My vision,
No fears, no destruction,
No death, no tears.
Imagine,
Imagine.

My vision,
No weapons, no bombs, no killing,
This we can all do,
No racist comments, no violence,
Imagine,
Imagine.

My vision,
We shall not fight on the beaches,
We shall not fight on the shores,
We shall not fight in this world,
Or any other,
Imagine,
Imagine.

My vision,
We'll all become one,
No fighting at all,
We can all become one,
Imagine,
That is my dream . . .

James Davis (12)
Woodbridge School, Woodbridge

I Believe

I believe in peace on Earth.
I believe in the impossible.
I believe in discovery.
I believe that the world can be changed.

We can make a difference,
No tears,
No fighting,
No war.
We can help the planet,
Live in peace
And harmony
And joy.

I believe that everyone has value.
I believe that everyone is equal.
I believe that you should not judge the people
You meet by the colour of their face
But treat them as your own.

We can make a difference,
No suffering,
No violence,
No war.

I believe that the world is ours to share
And we should not fight over land.
Every piece of land is as great as any other,
So why do we have to fight to survive
When every part of land is equal as everyone who lives in it?

I believe that the world can be changed,
And that is up to us.

Adam Lillywhite (11)
Woodbridge School, Woodbridge

I Have A Dream

You, the people of today,
Are the ones who have caused this problem,
And you are the ones that can sort it out.
Leave a better world for tomorrow.

If I was the last person on Earth,
I would bring every factory that pollutes,
Down to its knees,
To show what it had done to me.

Have you seen a polar bear?
You are lucky because, they soon
Won't be here,
Ice caps are melting everywhere,
To people who are trying to help,
This is unfair.

If I was the last person on Earth,
So that they would not get cut down or die,
I would guard every tree alone,
As if they were my own.

Have you heard about nuclear waste?
It is polluting our world,
So we must make haste.
It's in our seas and killing our fish,
Hurry up as we are being chased.

What colour do you want the world to be?
I don't want mine to be brown but green.

Louise Fraser (11)
Woodbridge School, Woodbridge

The Storm Of War

A storm is raging upon the sea.
And into this storm is crumbling,
Our land, our hope and all we hold dear.
It makes our people quake with fear,
But words are greater than war.

A storm is raging upon the sea.
The wind is a thousand grown men screaming,
With limbs missing, their bodies bleeding,
The storm looks down, its face jeering.
Yet words are greater than war.

A storm is raging upon the sea.
Its bloody carnage left behind,
The mangled bodies of innocent men.
Let's reshape this world, let's start again.
For words are greater than war.

A storm is raging upon the sea.
A storm of war upon the sea.
A storm started up by us.
A storm to be ended by us.
Because words can stop a war.

The storm is raging upon the sea.
My dream to stop the storm
Can work with all our help.
It's time to stop this war.
And words will stop this war!

Charlie Butt (12)
Woodbridge School, Woodbridge

End All War

I have a dream, hope and belief,
That war will end, life's worst thief.
It makes men die on home turf,
I will not stop until it is wiped off this Earth.

Evil armies rise against good,
Young men do what they should.
Many men fall for us,
So in return end war we must.

We are the sons of God, they the sons of the Devil,
Their only desire is to kill.
They come to us and attack,
Our last resort is to fight back

If you evil men are listening,
Stop your war, that dreadful thing.
War is for power and greed.
So stop your actions, all of us plead.

These evil men, who to Satan they pray,
Are like animals hunting down prey.
They raise their guns to our heads,
With no idea that blood will be shed.

Take a look at Mr Churchill,
Fought evil to stop that one kill.
If one day men like Hitler are no more,
That my friends, is the end to war.

Andrew Norman (12)
Woodbridge School, Woodbridge

Stop The War!

In our world there's lots of fear,
War and terror for all to hear.
On the news we see it all
People rise and people fall.

I have a dream,
A world at peace.
Where people love,
Where war has ceased.

The war has gone on for far too long,
Can't we go on like nothing's wrong?
Start afresh, a whole new Earth,
Let us see what it's really worth.

I have a dream,
A world at peace.
Where people love,
Where war has ceased.

I think it's time to show some love,
Open the heavens from above.
God didn't want the world like this,
Can't we live in heavenly bliss?

I have a dream,
A world at peace.
Where people love, where war has ceased.

Elliot Ashurst (12)
Woodbridge School, Woodbridge

I Have A Dream

This is for you, so don't ignore it.
We are the children of today,
We are the ones that can make the difference,
There is something we can all do.

We can end global warming,
We can stop the ice caps melting.
We can cure cancer,
This is your only warning.

We can help the poor,
And look after the elderly.
For that may be us some day,
You must abide this law.

Don't let the stomach of greed gobble you up,
Think about the people that are starving and parched,
Take what you need,
And I am sure that will be enough.

We can all walk that extra mile,
To save our amazing world.
So step up, come on,
Or you can add to that ungrateful pile.

Olivia Covell (12)
Woodbridge School, Woodbridge

The Future's Ours To Share

I have *a dream* of a peaceful world
Where Man could live life their own way,
Where children have no fear of being alone.

I have *a dream* of a cleaner world,
A place where rubbish doesn't clutter the ground,
And smoke doesn't darken the skies.

I have *a dream* of a friendly world,
Where kidnappings, murder and hate are just rumour,
Where drugs, poison and stealing are myth.

Yet when I wake up from this *dream* of mine,
I'm in a cruel, dirty, unfriendly world, that I know,
Is the real world, my home, my planet,
The place I wish to change, the home we all share.

I have *a dream* you all will help me,
Help me, share in the world, keep the world,
Help the world, help each other,
Don't ruin Earth and mankind.

The future's ours to share.

Catherine Cooper (12)
Woodbridge School, Woodbridge

The Future Is Now

The future of Earth is here and now;
It depends on every one of you here,
I know you may not believe quite how,
We are destroying our atmosphere!

The future of Earth is in our hands,
If we do not change very soon,
If nobody changes in all the lands,
For the Earth it will spell certain doom.

But my friends, if we work together,
We can change our evil ways,
We can save the Earth, maybe forever,
And keep alive those beautiful days.

When you leave this place my friends,
Keep in mind what you have heard today,
And please, can you make amends,
To this beautiful planet, on which we play.

James Budden (12)
Woodbridge School, Woodbridge

Tomorrow's Generation

When you get a moment, just ask yourself this,
Would the world be a better place if everyone was like you?
Do you plant trees, or cut them down?
Do you start fires, or put them out?
Do you fight crime, or help the wrongdoers?
Do you give to the poor, or take what little they have?
Do you preserve life, or take it away?
Have you done all that you can today
To make this world a better place?
We are tomorrow's generation; we can and will make things better
When you get a moment, just ask yourself this,
Would the world be a better place if everyone was like you?

Adele Macpherson (12)
Woodbridge School, Woodbridge

Think, Dream, Change, Poverty

Think, thinking, thought.
Dream, dreaming, dreamt.
Change, changing, changed.

Think of young and old, all suffer.
Thinking how we eat our tea and supper.
Thought: can we help them?

Dream to stop it all, the dreadful thing.
Dreaming to make life and people sing.
Dreamt: we can stop it!

Change the way we live today
Changing our world to make their way
Changed: someone's life!

Think, thinking, thought.
Dream, dreaming, dreamt.
Change, changing, changed.

Molly Fuller (12)
Woodbridge School, Woodbridge

I Had A Dream

I had a dream that the world was wrong, that it was rotten to the
Core, that it could not survive. While poverty and strife were rife.
That while brother killed brother in arms, and while people did
Others harm. But if people start to listen.
And sort themselves out
Then even Hell would freeze over.
And peace would spread to all.
From the seven rings of Hell
To the highest point of Heaven
And that would be swell.

I had a dream that the world was wrong,
But it is going to be put right
Mother, brother, father, sister,
All the same to work for what's right.
All the same to work for what's right.

Benedict Lelijveld (12)
Woodbridge School, Woodbridge

Young Writers Information

We hope you have enjoyed reading this book - and that you will continue to enjoy it in the coming years.

If you like reading and writing poetry drop us a line, or give us a call, and we'll send you a free information pack.

Alternatively if you would like to order further copies of this book or any of our other titles, then please give us a call or log onto our website at www.youngwriters.co.uk

Young Writers Information
Remus House
Coltsfoot Drive
Peterborough
PE2 9JX
(01733) 890066